Chakr

Unfolding India's Potential

Utkarsh Luthra

Dedicated to

My Family

Table of Content

The clock's hands had crept past midnight, and the world around Parth was a stark canvas of crimson and shadow. His own hands, painted in the gruesome hues of blood, were a constant, horrifying reminder of the incomprehensible event that had transpired. The distant streetlights cast a feeble orange glow, their light diluted and eerie, as if the very air itself was stained with the residue of tragedy. Parth's gaze, vacant and haunted, searched the starless sky above, a silent plea for answers etched across his blood-streaked face. But the heavens remained indifferent, offering no solace or explanation for the horror that had unfolded.

The once-bustling road now lay deserted, a barren expanse devoid of any human presence save for a lone figure huddled a few feet away. The beggar, a spectral apparition cloaked in tattered rags and a worn blanket, stared at Parth with an unsettling intensity. His eyes, dark and fathomless, reflected the ghastly scene like pools of obsidian.

A sudden, discordant sound shattered the silence, a chilling dissonance that echoed through the empty street. The beggar's head snapped towards the source, his gaunt features contorted in a grotesque mask of fear. Parth's gaze fell to his own feet, a flicker of recognition sparking in his tormented mind. The remnants of a once-innocent treat, a half-melted ice cream cone, lay discarded on the pavement, its sticky sweetness now a bitter reminder of the shattered innocence that stained his hands.

As Parth's eyes met the beggar's averted gaze, a wave of despair washed over him. The orange glow of the streetlights seemed to morph into a sickly yellow, and the distant blare of a car horn grew fainter with each passing second. The world around him blurred, his senses dulled by the encroaching darkness. And then, with a final, shuddering breath, Parth's eyelids fluttered closed, and the relentless cacophony of his mind finally fell silent.

Preface

If there is anything which inspires me the most, it is conversation. I love being part of conversations which are engaging, heated, cold, or even just a revelation. If there's anything I hate, it's conversation which is repetitive. So, this book is definitely not going to be about repetitive conversations between you and me. Well, that being said, I must say that there will be a lot of parts in the book which you might feel like they're repeating themselves, and I assure you that it is done very purposefully.

The world we inhabit today is woven with intricate threads of both darkness and light. That's the basic understanding we have of life. Where there is light, there will be shadows. If there are no shadows, there is no light. Point being, this contrasting nature is what makes the world whatever it is. It is a world teeming with opportunities, yet marred by deep-seated challenges. It is a world where dreams soar high, yet aspirations are often crushed beneath the weight of societal expectations. It is a world that desperately needs voices to illuminate its complexities, to challenge its norms, and to ignite sparks of change.

This book, born from a confluence of personal experiences, observations, and reflections, is my humble attempt to contribute to this ongoing conversation. It is an exploration of the human spirit's resilience in the face of adversity, a testament to the transformative power of hope and determination. It is an invitation to question, to challenge, and to dream.

The title "Chakr" is a powerful metaphor for the cyclical nature of challenges and opportunities in India's journey toward progress. The word "Chakr" (meaning "wheel" in Hindi) symbolizes the continuous cycle of problems and solutions that the country faces, particularly in the realms of healthcare, education, governance, and societal transformation.

Just as a wheel turns, moving forward while sometimes revisiting the same points, India's development is marked by recurring issues that need to be addressed and overcome in new ways. The book "Chakr:

Unfolding India's Potential" reflects this idea by exploring how these cycles have shaped the country's present and how breaking these cycles can lead to a brighter future.

"Chakr" also evokes the image of the Ashoka Chakra on India's national flag, representing the eternal wheel of law and dharma, symbolizing progress and righteousness. By choosing this title, the book connects India's past, present, and future, emphasizing the importance of continuous effort, resilience, and innovative thinking to unfold the nation's full potential.

Throughout the book, you'll also notice various references from Indian mythology, especially from the Mahabharat and Ramayan. The title "Chakr" also draws a profound connection to the Sudarshan Chakra, the legendary weapon wielded by Lord Vishnu in Hindu mythology. The Sudarshan Chakra is not just a symbol of power but also of protection, righteousness, and the ability to cut through chaos and restore order.

In the context of the book "Chakr: Unfolding India's Potential," the Sudarshan Chakra represents the sharp, decisive action needed to address the deeply entrenched problems within India's healthcare, education, and governance systems. Just as the Sudarshan Chakra is used to defeat evil and restore balance, the book advocates for cutting through the complexities and challenges that hinder India's progress, aiming to bring clarity and direction.

The connection to the Sudarshan Chakra reinforces the idea that India's potential can be fully realized only through decisive and righteous action. It symbolizes the need for powerful, transformative change to break the cycle of issues that the country faces. By invoking the Sudarshan Chakra, the book underscores the importance of not just recognizing the problems but actively working towards eliminating them with precision and purpose, much like how the Sudarshan Chakra eradicates obstacles in its path.

At its core, this narrative weaves together the stories of Parth, a young man grappling with the disillusionment of a flawed education system and the aftermath of a life-altering accident, embarking on a journey of self-discovery and purpose. The storyline is a complementary to the major topics and themes of the book.

The story, intertwined with the lives of countless others they encounter along the way, paint a vivid portrait of the challenges and opportunities that abound in India today. It is a land of stark contrasts, where ancient traditions coexist with modern aspirations, where dreams collide with harsh realities, and where the human spirit constantly strives to transcend its limitations.

I have a strong belief that we are all just copies creating copies of copies. Basically, there's no possibility of an "original creation." It's all just a bunch of influences which merge and fix together. Hence, inspired by various amazing thinkers, the book is divided into four sections, each drawing inspiration from a classic novel, fables and legends that carry a profound message. From the dystopian warnings of Brave New World to the timeless wisdom of the Bhagavad Gita, these literary echoes add depth and resonance to the narrative, while also keeping you, the readers, hopefully gripped to explore universal themes of human experience, societal structures, and the enduring quest for meaning and purpose. These are books very close to my heart. And each chapter and section embodies a theme which connects towards an independent block of the entire puzzle.

Section 1, titled The Plague, inspired by the novel written by Albert Camus, delves into the complexities of the healthcare system in India, exposing its glaring inequalities and the struggles faced by those on the margins of society. It unveils a system besieged by a multitude of challenges, from inadequate infrastructure and resource scarcity to the commercialization of healthcare and the erosion of patient-doctor relationships. The section sheds light on the plight of patients navigating a labyrinth of bureaucratic hurdles, the overburdened healthcare workers striving to deliver quality care amidst limited resources, and the ethical dilemmas that arise when profit-making takes precedence over patient welfare. The section lays bare the human cost of a broken healthcare system and calls for urgent reforms to ensure equitable access to healthcare for all.

Section 2, Fahrenheit 451, inspired by Ray Bradbury's novel, turns its focus on the education system, highlighting its limitations and its failure to nurture the true potential of its students. It delves deeper into the pressures faced by young people, exploring the suffocating weight of academic expectations, the narrow focus on standardized tests, and the erosion of critical thinking skills. The section exposes the chasm between the ivory towers of academia and the realities of the job market, highlighting the mismatch between the skills taught in classrooms and the demands of the modern workplace. The section unveils the disillusionment, frustration, and ultimately, the resilience of a generation caught between the pursuit of academic excellence and the search for personal fulfillment.

Section 3, Kalam's Vision, is a celebration of the boundless opportunities and potential that India offers. It draws inspiration from the life and teachings of Dr. APJ Abdul Kalam, the visionary scientist and former President of India, who believed in the power of dreams and the potential of the youth to transform the nation.

Kalam's legacy serves as a guiding star, illuminating the path towards a brighter future for India. This section delves into the myriad challenges that the country faces, from poverty and inequality to environmental degradation and social unrest. Yet, amidst these challenges, it also highlights the remarkable resilience and innovative spirit of the Indian people. It showcases the stories of ordinary citizens who have risen above adversity to become agents of change, inspiring others to follow in their footsteps.

The section emphasizes the importance of education, not just as a means to acquire knowledge, but as a tool for empowerment and social transformation. It highlights the role of technology and innovation in driving economic growth and improving the quality of life for all. It underscores the significance of inclusivity, diversity, and social justice in building a harmonious and equitable society.

Ultimately, this section seeks to inspire hope and optimism, reminding us of the immense potential that lies within India. It celebrates the diversity of its people, the richness of its culture, and the indomitable spirit that has defined its history. It calls upon the youth to embrace their role as torchbearers of the nation's future, to dream big, and to work tirelessly towards realizing the vision of a New India.

Finally, Section 4, The Road Ahead, contemplates the future, exploring themes of personal growth, resilience, and the unwavering pursuit of one's dreams. It challenges readers to break free from societal constraints, embrace change, and forge their own paths towards a fulfilling and meaningful life. The section delves deeper into the concept of metamorphosis, examining how individuals can transform their lives by overcoming adversity, embracing challenges, and cultivating a growth mindset. It highlights the importance of self-awareness, resilience, and the ability to adapt to changing circumstances. The section also explores the role of mentorship, support systems, and the power of community in fostering personal growth and development.

Through the lens of Parth's journey, the section showcases the transformative power of education, not just in acquiring knowledge, but in shaping one's worldview and empowering individuals to become agents of change. It emphasizes the importance of lifelong learning, critical thinking, and the ability to navigate an increasingly complex and interconnected world.

Ultimately, this section offers a message of hope and inspiration, reminding readers that the future is not predetermined but shaped by the choices we make. It encourages readers to embrace their potential, to pursue their passions, and to contribute to a better world. By embracing change, overcoming challenges, and cultivating a growth mindset, individuals can unlock their full potential and create a brighter future for themselves and for generations to come.

I will proudly say that this book is a book of problems. It highlights the society's very well known, well documented problems in a set manner which doesn't really create enough meaning, except, it starts a conversation. A conversation, more important than anything else, within the readers. It's about framing and getting to the gist of these problems with great care.

Through the pages of this book, I invite you to embark on a journey of self-discovery, to question the status quo, and to envision a world that is both just and equitable. If you allow me to be a bit dramatic, this book is more than just a collection of words; it is a call to action, a catalyst for change. It is a testament to the resilience of the human spirit and the power of hope to illuminate even the darkest corners of our world. But well, in its essence, it's a scream into the echo chamber, hoping eventually to not be the only one hearing the noise.

As you turn the pages, may you find within yourself the courage to dream, the strength to persevere, and the wisdom to navigate the complexities of life. May this book be a source of inspiration, a companion on your journey, and a catalyst for positive change.

Ultimately, between all the problems and solutions, this book is a celebration of the human spirit, a testament to our capacity for growth, and a vision of a future filled with endless possibilities. It is a reminder that we are all interconnected, and that our actions have the power to ripple through generations to come.

This book is for you, dear reader. It is a gift, a challenge, and an invitation to join the movement for a better world, which starts by accepting issues. May it ignite a spark within you, a flame that burns brightly and illuminates the path ahead.

This book is for you. I hope you find it both enlightening and empowering.

Acknowledgement

Embarking on the journey of writing a book is akin to navigating a vast and uncharted ocean, where the currents of inspiration and the tides of self-doubt intertwine in a perpetual dance. It is a solitary endeavor, yet one that is profoundly shaped by the countless individuals who have touched our lives, ignited our passions, and nurtured our dreams.

As I stand on the precipice of this literary voyage, my heart overflows with gratitude for the multitude of souls who have contributed, directly or indirectly, to the creation of this book. Their presence, their wisdom, their unwavering support, have been the guiding stars that illuminated my path, the anchors that held me steady amidst the stormy seas of doubt and uncertainty.

First and foremost, I extend my deepest gratitude to my family, the bedrock of my existence. To my parents, whose unconditional love and unwavering belief in my abilities have been my constant source of strength and inspiration. To my sister, Shivanshi, whose companionship, laughter, and shared experiences have enriched my life in countless ways. To my extended family, whose collective wisdom and unwavering support have been a source of comfort and encouragement throughout this journey.

I would especially like to thank Neha, for her absolute support in the writing process and thorough first readings including every chapter's focus and theme connectivity. You've been nothing short of the best support system I could have in the writing process.

I would also like to especially thank Ayush and Ansh from my Medoc Health team for their constant presence in writing this book. It's impossible for me to manage my workload and day, let alone write an entire book, without the support of both of you.

I am also deeply indebted to my mentors and teachers, whose guidance and wisdom have shaped my intellectual and creative pursuits. To all my teachers who instilled in me a love for learning and a thirst for knowledge. To my colleagues and peers, whose insights and collaborations have broadened my horizons and challenged me to think critically and creatively. To the countless authors and thinkers whose works have ignited my imagination and fueled my passion for storytelling.

I would also like to express my appreciation to the countless individuals who have shared their stories with me, whose experiences have informed and enriched this narrative. To the patients and healthcare workers I encountered during my research, whose resilience and compassion in the face of adversity moved me deeply. To the students and educators who shared their struggles and triumphs within the education system, whose voices echoed the challenges and aspirations of a generation. To the entrepreneurs and innovators who dared to dream big and create a better future,whose stories inspired me to believe in the power of human ingenuity.

I am grateful to the countless friends and supporters who have cheered me on, offered words of encouragement, and patiently listened to my endless ramblings about plot twists and character arcs. To my writing group, whose constructive feedback and unwavering support have been invaluable throughout this process. To my editor, whose keen eye and insightful suggestions have helped me refine my prose and elevate my storytelling.

This book is a testament to the collective spirit of humanity, a celebration of our shared experiences and our enduring quest for meaning and purpose. It is a reflection of the world we inhabit, a mirror held up to our triumphs and our failings, our hopes and our fears.

As you embark on this literary journey, may you find within these pages a reflection of your own experiences, a source of inspiration, and a renewed sense of hope for the future. May this book spark conversations, ignite passions, and encourage us all to strive for a world where compassion, empathy, and justice prevail.

The Plague

"There's no question of heroism in all this. It's a matter of common decency. That's an idea which may make some people smile, but the only means of fighting a plague is - common decency."

- Albert Camus in The Plague

The Inferno

Parth's eyelids fluttered open, the world a disorienting blur of shadows and flashing lights. The rhythmic sway of the vehicle, coupled with the muffled drone of the engine, sent waves of nausea through his battered body. He caught a fleeting glimpse of the van's interior, its dimly lit space casting an ominous pall over the scene. Through the grime-streaked windows, the streetlights danced and flickered, their reflections morphing into grotesque shapes that seemed to mock his fragile state. Panic surged through him, and with a strangled gasp, he succumbed once more to the comforting embrace of unconsciousness.

When Parth's eyes opened again, he found himself in a realm that mirrored the horrors of Dante's Inferno, yet eerily devoid of compassion or care. The hospital ward was a grotesque tableau of human suffering, a cacophony of despair that assaulted his senses from all sides, shrouded in a perpetual twilight of neglect. The air hung heavy with the pungent stench of sweat, antiseptic, and decay, a nauseating symphony that clung to the back of his throat. The feeble fluorescent lights, their bulbs long past their prime, cast a dim and flickering glow on the scene, obscuring the full extent of the agony within.

Beds lined the walls, crammed together with barely enough space for a whisper to pass between them. Each one held a story of pain and desperation, seemingly forgotten amidst the indifferent hum of the understaffed ward. A chorus of moans, coughs, and labored breaths filled the air, punctuated by the occasional sharp cry of agony, yet met with only the distant murmur of conversation from the overworked nurses' station. A skeletal figure, his skin stretched taut over jutting bones, lay gasping for air, his chest heaving with each agonizing inhale, his pleas for help going unanswered. A young woman, her face contorted in a silent scream, clutched at her swollen belly, her body wracked with waves of unrelenting pain, tears streaming down her cheeks unnoticed. An elderly man, his eyes vacant and lifeless, stared

Let's start breaking things down. I have very limited space in this book and wish to have a very clear conversation here. As I write this book, I want you to disagree with me, in principle and in practice. There needs to be a fair amount of disagreement for actually making sure that we are in the capacity to actually appreciate whatever we have here. The objective of the book is to ensure clarity and bring perspective to some things and voice to the other.

As the founder of Medoc Health, we work very deeply in solving problems of healthcare. I've talked to hundreds of doctors, nurses, hospital administrators, healthcare workers, NGOs among every other stakeholder, especially patients and their families. Hence, it is very evident that the first thing I want to start this conversation with is Healthcare.

Other than my personal bias towards the industry with the stories I have of various people I've met in the industry, the major reason why the first thing I wanted to discuss ways Healthcare is mainly for two reasons:

First of all, in the intricate history of human existence, health stands as the most precious thread, holding together the fabric of our lives, quite literally. A nation's well-being is inextricably linked to the health of its citizens, and the provision of quality healthcare is not merely a moral imperative, but a strategic investment in its future.

India, a nation of over 1.4 billion people, faces a unique set of healthcare challenges, its vast and diverse population grappling with a complex interplay of socioeconomic, cultural, and environmental factors. There are so many races, castes, and societal barries in the nation. I would first of all start with saying that the system that we have built to this date around healthcare is definitely worthy of being a case study across the world. With achievements like the distribution of vaccines to managing large-scale media campaigns, at scale, the Indian healthcare system is marvelous.

But, sadly, the statistics of the ground levels paint a sobering picture. Getting straight to the problems now, despite significant progress in recent years, India's healthcare expenditure as a percentage of GDP remains alarmingly low, hovering around a mere 4% in 2024. Why is this so concerning? Because as a growing nation, robust healthcare is the foundation of our nation. It ensures security of the citizens on every level. The healthcare of our nation is just as maintaining democracy.

This expenditure pales in comparison to developed nations, where healthcare spending often exceeds 10% of GDP. The consequences of this underinvestment are evident in the stark disparities in health outcomes across the country. While urban areas boast a relatively robust healthcare infrastructure, rural communities often grapple with a severe shortage of facilities and qualified personnel.

And secondly, because it's the most important thing to anyone. As it is very obvious, nothing is more important than one's health. And yet, the most compromised asset that we look at is our own health. With the rise of capitalism, the care for health across the country has gone to shambles. Today, even if someone wishes to lead a healthy life, the challenges one has to face are extreme.

The rise of private healthcare, while offering state-of-the-art facilities and specialized care, has also exacerbated existing inequalities, creating a two-tiered system that favors the affluent. This needs to change.

The high cost of private healthcare remains a formidable barrier for the majority of the population, who are forced to rely on the overburdened and under-resourced public sector. This has led to a situation where millions of Indians are unable to access the medications and treatments they need, resulting in delayed diagnosis, inadequate care, and preventable deaths.

It is naturally the understanding that it's easier to navigate the labyrinth, than the world of public and private healthcare, examining the disparities in access and affordability, the ethical dilemmas faced by healthcare professionals, and the urgent need for system reforms.

Let me give you a summary of the entire industry. So, here's a crash course on Indian Healthcare System:

The state of Indian healthcare is a stark juxtaposition of the nation's burgeoning economic progress and its deep-seated social inequalities. While India boasts of being the world's fastest-growing major economy, its healthcare system remains a woefully inadequate and deeply fractured entity, leaving hundreds of millions of its citizens vulnerable to preventable diseases, disability, and premature death.

The numbers tell a harrowing tale. India's public healthcare spending, at a mere 1.5% of its GDP, is among the lowest in the world. This chronic underfunding translates into a severe shortage of healthcare infrastructure, particularly in rural areas where over 65% of the population resides.

The country's doctor-to-patient ratio, at 1:1,456, falls far short of the WHO's recommended standard of 1:1,000. This scarcity of medical professionals, coupled with a lack of trained nurses and paramedics, results in overburdened hospitals, long waiting times, and compromised patient care.

A staggering 70% of healthcare expenditure in India is out-of-pocket, forcing millions into poverty each year. The lack of comprehensive health insurance coverage leaves the vast majority of the population exposed to the financial devastation of unexpected illness or injury.

Beyond the cold statistics, the reality of India's healthcare crisis is perhaps best illustrated through the lived experiences of its citizens. If you think it's too many numbers, the summary is, and I'll be deliberately repeating, that we do not have enough doctors and the facilities we have right now are not enough. Public Healthcare is currently not supportive to the middle class taxpayer anymore and there is a major concern.

When we talk about accessibility and inclusivity, recently, my team told me about the story of a farmer from a remote village in Uttar Pradesh. When his young daughter fell critically ill, the nearest hospital was over 50 kilometers away. The lack of affordable transportation and the exorbitant cost of private healthcare forced him to rely on unqualified quacks, ultimately leading to his daughter's tragic demise. There are endless such stories forming every single day. And the problem is beyond just hospital access.

And guess what, even in the bustling cities like Chandigarh, Delhi and Mumbai, the situation is hardly better. Overcrowded public hospitals, with patients often sharing beds or lying on the floor, are a common sight. The lack of basic hygiene and sanitation in these facilities poses a serious risk of infection, further compounding the patients' woes.

Recently, one of my close friends got into an accident and the closest hospital we could find, unfortunately, was a Civil Hospital. On entering the hospital, the scenario was extremely horrible. There were people on the floor even. The bed on which they treated the patient had stains of flesh blood from another patient and the waiting area was not even sanitary, forget sterile.

Even in the relatively affluent urban centers, access to quality healthcare remains a privilege for the few. The high cost of private healthcare, coupled with long waiting lists for specialized treatment, forces many middle-class families to compromise on their health or deplete their savings. This has in turn created various clinics and micro private practices which provide quick relief to the patient at the risk of worse complications because of no investigations.

The disparity in healthcare access between urban and rural areas is particularly glaring. While major cities boast of state-of-the-art private hospitals catering to the affluent, rural areas are often left with dilapidated government clinics manned by overworked and underpaid staff. I have a deeper dive on this in the further chapter, but I wish to clarify on how important this part of the conversation is.

The crisis in Indian healthcare also takes a heavy toll on its healthcare professionals. Doctors, nurses, and paramedics are often overworked, underpaid, and lacking essential resources. The stress and burnout are palpable, leading to a decline in morale and a brain drain of talented medical professionals to developed countries. What's worse? They aren't even respected enough.

India today has a shortage of nursing staff and yet, I've had conversations with various nurses who have reported on how even their own families don't understand or respect their work. In my research, I came across several nursing staff which clearly mentioned how there have been cases of sexual eve teasing and objectification from patients itself.

As for doctors, if you think they're very respected in Indian society, the words and actions have a difference and as around 70% doctors have reported some form of physical violence in their profession. They've reported how they're overworked and underpaid, and yet, assumed by society to be printing money. I'll get on the education aspect of things later.

Violence and abuse against healthcare professionals is a growing concern in India. Verbal abuse, threats, and even physical assaults on doctors and nurses are becoming increasingly common, especially in emergency departments and overcrowded public hospitals.

This creates a hostile and unsafe work environment for healthcare professionals, adding to their stress and anxiety. The fear of violence and abuse can also deter young people from entering the healthcare profession, further exacerbating the human resource crisis.

This violence, like you may expect as educated readers, doesn't come from sects of our society which are underrepresented or are known for their aggressions. These come from well-mannered, educated individuals. These are a result of lack of understanding across the population on how medicine works.

Doctors are treated as God, and at a moment of loss or perceivable loss, it is understandable to lose faith even in God. But we need to, for once, drop doctors from that pedestal, because doctors are human beings too. The scope for human error exists and there is no way that can be resolved unless there is significant development in technology to cover for the same. And that development is impossible with the budgets and funds available in public healthcare.

Sadly, while writing this book's final manuscript itself, I came across the news of a rape case of a female resident doctor while she was on-duty. It brings through various questions and blurs the entire society as a whole with clear questions. Moreover, it asks us to question the basic security and requirements of even the healthcare workers are not satiable by the authorities, hence, questioning various stakeholders.

So, where do we start at addressing the administrative issues?

India's healthcare system is plagued by a severe infrastructure deficit, a critical issue that undermines its ability to deliver effective and accessible care to its vast population. Doctors on-call don't even have on-call rooms. From dilapidated hospitals and clinics to a lack of essential medical equipment, the infrastructure crisis in Indian healthcare is a stark reality that affects patients and healthcare professionals alike.

I recently went to a very popular hospital in the state and what I saw was unsanitary treatment of people in the middle of a huge city, at the heart of the state as if it's a military camp with refugees and soldiers.

A significant portion of India's healthcare infrastructure is in a state of disrepair. Many government hospitals and clinics, particularly in rural areas, are dilapidated and overcrowded, lacking basic amenities such as clean water, sanitation, and proper ventilation.

Patients are often forced to share beds or lie on the floor, compromising their dignity and increasing the risk of infection. The lack of adequate space and resources also hampers the ability of healthcare professionals to provide quality care, leading to delays in treatment, misdiagnosis, and even preventable deaths.

As a matter of fact, there was this one incident around a year ago when my roommate fell ill and we thought let's take him to a hospital, and, given the closeness of the Civil Hospital, we entered there. To our surprise, the Emergency room and General ward were a mess.

A similar incident happened when I got into a minor accident recently and was required to get my wound dressed. After visiting the Civil Hospital, again because of proximity, on my second visit to another doctor, I had to get the dressing changed and the nurse was in shock at the way the dressing was done. It took us 10 extra minutes and burning pain to just get it off.

The shortage of essential medical equipment is another critical issue plaguing Indian healthcare. Many hospitals and clinics, especially in rural areas, lack basic diagnostic tools such as X-ray machines, ultrasound scanners, and blood testing facilities. This forces patients to travel long distances or rely on expensive private diagnostic centers, further adding to their financial burden.

The lack of advanced medical equipment such as ventilators, dialysis machines, and intensive care units is particularly acute in smaller towns and rural areas. This leaves patients with critical illnesses or injuries with limited options for treatment, often resulting in tragic consequences.

The disparity in healthcare infrastructure between urban and rural areas is a glaring reality in India. While major cities boast of state-of-the-art private hospitals catering to the affluent, rural areas are often left with dilapidated government clinics manned by overworked and underpaid staff.

This urban-rural divide creates a two-tiered healthcare system, where those living in rural areas are disproportionately affected by the lack of access to quality healthcare. The long distances to reach hospitals, coupled with the lack of affordable transportation, further exacerbate the problem.

The shortage of trained healthcare professionals is another major challenge facing the Indian healthcare system. Repeating the statistic again, a country with 25 lakh NEET aspirants every year, the country's doctor-to-patient ratio, at 1:1,456, falls far short of the WHO's recommended standard of 1:1,000. This scarcity of medical professionals, particularly specialists, is particularly acute in rural areas.

The shortage of doctors and specialists is a multifaceted problem rooted in various factors. The limited number of medical colleges and seats, coupled with the high cost of medical education, restricts the number of students who can pursue a career in medicine.

The brain drain of talented medical professionals to developed countries, lured by better pay and working conditions, and more importantly because of better fee structures than colleges in India further exacerbates the shortage. The lack of adequate infrastructure and resources in rural areas also discourages doctors from practicing in these areas, leaving them underserved.

I came across a rather interesting encounter with a doctor recently. He was trained in the United States of America with all kinds of laurels. He even wrote a lot of research papers and articles and everything. He came back to India to set up his own hospital in Neurology. The complete brand value of that hospital came from his education from the US. In my conversation with him, he very frankly revealed how there were multiple instances when he actually felt that working in a hospital in the US has a better scope of comfort. His motivation to come to India was mostly around his family and set-up, but according to his insights, India, in itself, has a great scope of growth in Healthcare. In every way.

The shortage of trained nurses and paramedics is another critical issue affecting the quality of healthcare in India. Nurses play a vital role in patient care, providing essential support to doctors and ensuring the smooth functioning of hospitals and clinics.

However, the nursing profession in India is often undervalued and underpaid, leading to a shortage of qualified nurses.The lack of adequate training facilities and career advancement opportunities further discourages young people from entering the profession.

The shortage of paramedics, who provide emergency medical care in pre-hospital settings, is equally concerning. The lack of trained paramedics can lead to delays in treatment and increased mortality rates, particularly in rural areas where access to hospitals is limited.

Addressing the infrastructure and human resource crises in Indian healthcare will require a multi-pronged approach involving increased public spending, policy reforms, and innovative solutions.

The cornerstone of a robust healthcare system lies in adequate financial backing. India's current public healthcare expenditure, hovering around a meager 1.28% of its GDP, is woefully insufficient to address the nation's vast and diverse healthcare needs. A significant increase in public spending is imperative to fuel the transformation of the healthcare landscape.

Building new hospitals and clinics, especially in underserved rural and remote areas, is crucial to expanding access to care. Equally important is the modernization and upgrading of existing facilities to ensure they are equipped to handle the growing demand and provide quality services. This includes revamping dilapidated structures, improving sanitation and hygiene, and expanding capacity to reduce overcrowding.

Equipping healthcare facilities with state-of-the-art diagnostic and treatment tools is paramount. This includes investing in basic equipment like X-ray machines, ultrasound scanners, and laboratory facilities, as well as advanced technologies such as MRI machines, CT scanners, and critical care equipment. Ensuring a steady supply of essential medicines and consumables is also vital to avoid disruptions in patient care.

India faces a critical shortage of skilled healthcare workers, including doctors, nurses, and paramedics. Increased public spending should be allocated to expanding medical education and training programs, improving the quality of training,and providing ongoing professional development opportunities. This will not only address the current shortage but also ensure a steady pipeline of qualified healthcare professionals for the future.

Other than this, While financial investment is crucial, it must be complemented by comprehensive policy reforms to address the systemic challenges in the healthcare sector. These reforms should focus on key areas that directly impact the accessibility and quality of care. Revamping medical education is essential to produce competent and compassionate healthcare professionals. This includes increasing the number of medical colleges and seats, improving the curriculum to focus on practical skills and patient-centric care, and ensuring rigorous standards for accreditation and licensing. Making medical education more accessible and affordable, especially for students from marginalized communities, is also crucial to building a diverse and representative healthcare workforce.

Incentivizing doctors to practice in rural areas is vital to bridge the urban-rural healthcare divide. This can be achieved through a combination of financial incentives, such as higher salaries and allowances, and non-financial incentives, such as improved infrastructure, housing, and educational opportunities for their families. Creating a supportive and conducive work environment in rural areas is also key to attracting and retaining healthcare professionals.

Enhancing the status and remuneration of nurses and paramedics is crucial to attract and retain talent in these vital professions. This includes improving their working conditions, providing opportunities for career advancement, and recognizing their contributions to patient care. Strengthening nursing and paramedic education and training programs is also essential to ensure a skilled and competent workforce.

No industry or field of work can grow without continuous development. Embracing innovation and technology is key to overcoming the challenges of delivering healthcare in a vast and diverse country like India. Several innovative solutions can help bridge the gap in healthcare access, particularly in remote and underserved areas.

Deploying mobile health clinics equipped with basic diagnostic and treatment facilities can bring healthcare services directly to the doorsteps of underserved communities. These clinics can provide preventive care, screenings, and basic treatment for common ailments, reducing the burden on hospitals and improving health outcomes.

Collaborations between the government and private sector can leverage the strengths of both to improve healthcare delivery. Public-private partnerships can facilitate the sharing of resources, expertise, and technology, leading to more efficient and effective healthcare services.

In conclusion, addressing the complex challenges of India's healthcare system requires a multi-faceted approach that combines increased public spending, policy reforms, and innovative solutions. By prioritizing these key areas, India can build a robust and equitable healthcare system that ensures access to quality care for all its citizens, regardless of their location or socioeconomic status. The road to healthcare reform may be long and arduous, but the journey is essential to secure the health and well-being of the nation and its people.

The challenges are immense, but the stakes are too high to ignore. The health of a nation is its greatest wealth, and India cannot afford to neglect this vital asset any longer. It is time to act decisively to build a robust and equitable healthcare system that ensures the health and well-being of all its citizens.

One of the most pressing challenges faced by healthcare professionals in India is the relentless pressure of overwork. Long hours, demanding shifts, and a constant stream of patients leave them physically and mentally exhausted. Doctors, especially those in public hospitals and rural areas, often work 12-14 hour shifts, sometimes even longer during emergencies or outbreaks.

This chronic overwork leads to burnout, a state of emotional, physical, and mental exhaustion characterized by feelings of cynicism, detachment, and a reduced sense of accomplishment. Burnout not only affects the well-being of healthcare professionals but also compromises patient care. Studies have shown that burnout is associated with increased medical errors, decreased patient satisfaction, and higher rates of physician turnover.

I have seen firsthand how medical negligence can be fatal. And it's not just a number for someone. A simple and thorough medical history along with basic investigations alone can contribute to 35-40% cases not getting fatal.

Despite their crucial role in society, many healthcare professionals in India are grossly underpaid. Salaries for doctors, nurses, and paramedics, especially those in the public sector, are often meager and fail to reflect the demanding nature of their work and the high level of skill and expertise required. This lack of sufficient compensation leaves various doctors with no choice but to opt for a multiple earning model hence working extra hours and stretch themselves which again contributes to the vicious cycle of stress and fatigue.

Moreover, this financial insecurity can be particularly demoralizing for young professionals who have invested years of their lives and significant resources in their education and training. The low salaries are still hardly ever discouraging most talented individuals from pursuing a career in healthcare, but it does further exacerbate the shortage of qualified professionals.

As a cherry on the top, healthcare professionals in India often face a constant struggle due to a lack of essential resources and support. This includes a shortage of medical equipment, supplies, and even basic amenities such as clean water and sanitation in many hospitals and clinics. The lack of adequate infrastructure and technology can severely hamper the ability of healthcare professionals to provide timely and effective care. It can also lead to frustration and a sense of helplessness, as they are often forced to make do with limited resources or improvise solutions. The lack of support staff, such as nurses, paramedics, and technicians, further adds to the workload of doctors and nurses.This can lead to delays in treatment, missed diagnoses, and compromised patient safety.

Investing in healthcare professionals is not just a matter of fairness; it is a strategic imperative for building a robust and resilient healthcare system. By prioritizing their well-being and empowering them to deliver quality care, India can ensure the health and prosperity of its people for generations to come.

And I have not yet discussed the most crucial aspect of this discussion. Patients and their families.

In India, seeking healthcare is often an arduous journey fraught with challenges, delays, and financial burdens. Patients, especially those from marginalized communities and rural areas, face a multitude of obstacles in accessing timely, affordable, and quality care.

One of the most pervasive challenges faced by patients in India is the agonizingly long waiting times for consultations,diagnostics, and treatment. Overcrowded public hospitals, with their limited resources and staff, often struggle to cope with the overwhelming demand for healthcare services.

Patients, especially those with non-emergency conditions, can spend hours, if not days, waiting for their turn to see a doctor or undergo a simple procedure. This not only causes immense physical and mental distress but also disrupts their livelihoods and education.

These waiting hours are exactly what gave me the opportunity to actually talk to them. These families and patients, when approached sensitively, often discussed their problems and their situations. The healthcare industry pulls them out and exhausts them to the last drop.

The long waiting times also have a cascading effect, delaying diagnosis, treatment, and recovery. In some cases, the delay can be fatal, especially for patients with critical illnesses or injuries which are not yet discovered. While public healthcare facilities offer subsidized or free services, they are often plagued by overcrowding, long waiting times, and a lack of quality care. The high cost of healthcare in India is another major obstacle for patients, especially those from low-income backgrounds.

The dire situation of the public sector is what forces many patients to turn to private healthcare providers, where the cost of consultations, diagnostics, and treatment can be exorbitant, many a times even 30-40 times the fees they would have to pay in a public facility.

Access to quality healthcare remains a distant dream for many Indians, especially those living in rural areas and marginalized communities. The lack of qualified healthcare professionals, essential medical equipment, and basic infrastructure in these areas severely compromises the quality of care available.

Patients are often forced to rely on unqualified practitioners or traditional healers, putting their health at further risk. Misdiagnosis, inappropriate treatment, and complications are common, leading to increased morbidity and mortality rates.

Even in urban areas, the quality of care can vary significantly depending on the healthcare provider and the patient's ability to pay. The lack of standardized protocols, quality assurance mechanisms, and accountability in the healthcare system further erodes patient trust and confidence.

The disparity in healthcare access and quality between urban and rural areas is a stark reality in India. While major cities boast of state-of-the-art private hospitals and a concentration of specialized medical professionals, rural areas are often left with dilapidated government clinics and a severe shortage of qualified doctors and nurses.

This urban-rural divide creates a two-tiered healthcare system, where those living in rural areas are disproportionately affected by the lack of access to timely, affordable, and quality care. The long distances to reach hospitals, coupled with the lack of affordable transportation, further exacerbate the problem.

Mental health remains a neglected and stigmatized issue in India. The lack of awareness, social stigma, and limited access to mental healthcare services prevent many individuals from seeking help. The long waiting times, high costs, and lack of trained mental health professionals further compound the problem.

The consequences of untreated mental health conditions can be devastating, leading to social isolation, decreased productivity, and even suicide. The COVID-19 pandemic has further exacerbated the mental health crisis in India,highlighting the urgent need for increased investment in mental healthcare services and awareness campaigns to reduce stigma.

The challenges faced by patients in India's healthcare system are complex and multifaceted, requiring a concerted effort from the government, healthcare providers, and civil society to address. It is imperative to shift the focus from a provider-centric to a patient-centric approach, prioritizing the needs and experiences of patients at every step of their healthcare journey.

Increased public spending on healthcare, coupled with policy reforms aimed at improving infrastructure, human resources, and quality assurance, is crucial. Expanding health insurance coverage, promoting preventive care, and leveraging technology to bridge the urban-rural divide are also essential steps towards a more accessible, affordable, and equitable healthcare system.

Why is the healthcare system so messed up? Why, even after 78 years of Independence, we're still looking for covers around the budgets and excuses for the lack of development. Is the government not doing enough?

India's healthcare sector, despite its vast potential and the dedication of countless healthcare professionals, remains mired in a complex web of systemic issues. Corruption, inefficiency, and poor governance are deeply entrenched in the system, creating formidable barriers to access, affordability, and quality care. Let's briefly into these systemic challenges, exploring their root causes and devastating consequences, and highlighting the urgent need for comprehensive reform.

Corruption, like a malignant tumor, has infiltrated every level of India's healthcare system, from the highest echelons of policy-making to the grassroots level of service delivery. Bribery, kickbacks, and embezzlement of public funds are rampant, diverting resources away from essential healthcare services and undermining public trust.

The nexus between unscrupulous pharmaceutical companies, doctors, and diagnostic centers, often referred to as the "medical mafia," is a prime example of corruption in Indian healthcare. Doctors are often incentivized to prescribe unnecessary tests and medications, leading to overtreatment and inflated medical bills for patients. This practice not only exploits patients financially but also poses serious health risks due to the potential side effects of unnecessary medications and procedures. The "medical mafia" thrives on the lack of transparency and accountability in the healthcare system, perpetuating a vicious cycle of corruption and exploitation.

Inefficiency, fueled by bureaucratic red tape and a lack of coordination between various stakeholders, is another major challenge plaguing India's healthcare system. The convoluted processes for procurement, distribution, and utilization of resources often lead to delays, wastage, and suboptimal outcomes.

The recent COVID-19 pandemic exposed the glaring inefficiencies in India's healthcare system. The initial shortage of vaccines, despite the country being a major vaccine manufacturer, was attributed to a lack of foresight, poor planning, and bureaucratic hurdles. This resulted in a chaotic and inequitable vaccine rollout, with many vulnerable populations being left behind. The lack of a centralized and efficient system for vaccine distribution and administration further compounded the problem, highlighting the urgent need for streamlining processes and improving coordination.

Poor governance, characterized by a lack of accountability, transparency, and effective leadership, is a root cause of many systemic issues in India's healthcare system. The absence of clear policies, regulatory oversight, and performance monitoring mechanisms allows corruption and inefficiency to thrive.

Another interesting case is of the phenomenon of "ghost hospitals," where public funds are allocated for healthcare facilities that exist only on paper, which is a stark example of poor governance. These non-existent hospitals serve as conduits for embezzlement and misappropriation of public funds, depriving communities of essential healthcare services. The lack of accountability and transparency in the healthcare system allows such malpractices to persist, highlighting the urgent need for stronger regulatory oversight and performance monitoring mechanisms.

The systemic issues of corruption, inefficiency, and poor governance have a devastating impact on patients and society at large. The diversion of resources due to corruption and inefficiency results in a shortage of essential healthcare services,particularly in rural and underserved areas. This limits access to care for millions of Indians, especially those from marginalized communities. The lack of affordable healthcare options forces patients to rely on expensive private providers or resort to unqualified practitioners, leading to high out-of-pocket expenditure and financial hardship. The lack of accountability and transparency in the healthcare system allows substandard care and medical negligence to persist, jeopardizing patient safety and well-being. The rampant corruption and inefficiency in the healthcare system erode public trust and confidence, leading to a reluctance to seek care and a reliance on self-medication or traditional remedies.

While India's healthcare system faces daunting challenges, it is important to acknowledge the positive developments and rays of hope that offer a glimmer of a brighter future. From groundbreaking advances in medical technology to successful public health campaigns and the unwavering dedication of healthcare workers, these silver linings provide a counterpoint to the bleak reality and inspire optimism for a healthier India.

India has witnessed remarkable progress in medical technology in recent years, with innovations in diagnostics, treatment,and patient care transforming the healthcare landscape. From telemedicine and robotic surgery to artificial intelligence and 3D printing, these technological advancements are revolutionizing the way healthcare is delivered, making it more accessible, affordable, and effective.

Innovations in treatment, such as minimally invasive surgeries, targeted drug delivery systems, and robotic-assisted procedures, have improved patient outcomes and reduced recovery times. The growing adoption of telemedicine,particularly in the wake of the COVID-19 pandemic, has enabled remote consultations, diagnosis, and monitoring,bridging the gap between patients and healthcare providers in distant locations.

India has a rich history of successful public health campaigns that have significantly improved the health and well-being of its population. The Pulse Polio immunization program, launched in 1995, is a prime example of a successful public health initiative that has virtually eradicated polio from the country. Other notable campaigns include the National Tuberculosis Control Program, the National AIDS Control Program, and the Swachh Bharat Abhiyan (Clean India Mission). These campaigns have raised awareness, promoted preventive care, and improved access to treatment, contributing to a decline in the prevalence of these diseases.

Amidst the challenges and limitations, India's healthcare workers continue to demonstrate unwavering dedication and commitment to their profession. Doctors, nurses, and paramedics work tirelessly, often in difficult and demanding conditions, to provide care to their patients. Their resilience, compassion, and selflessness are an inspiration, reminding us of the human face of healthcare and the importance of recognizing and valuing their contributions. The COVID-19 pandemic has further highlighted the critical role of healthcare workers, who have risked their own lives to save others.

The Indian government has launched several initiatives aimed at improving the healthcare system, some of which have shown promise but are yet to make a significant impact.

Launched in 2018, Ayushman Bharat, also known as the Pradhan Mantri Jan Arogya Yojana (PMJAY), is the world's largest government-funded health insurance scheme. It aims to provide health coverage to over 500 million poor and vulnerable people, enabling them to access cashless treatment at empaneled hospitals. While the scheme has faced implementation challenges and concerns about its sustainability, it has the potential to significantly improve healthcare access for the poor. While I've had more than 80% of the doctors I've met clearly stating that they do not like the management of the facilities and the way the initiative is implemented, it's a relief to various families and just the sense of basic security to an individual is crucial sometimes like a ray of hope in the vast ocean.

Other than this, the NDHM aims to create a unified digital health ecosystem for India. It envisions a system where every citizen has a unique health ID, linked to their medical records,prescriptions, and diagnostic reports. This would enable seamless sharing of health information between healthcare providers, improve patient care, and facilitate research and policy-making. While the NDHM is still in its early stages, it has the potential to revolutionize healthcare delivery in India. As someone who works closely with NDHM, I assure you that it's an initiative that will surely open doors for everyone.

Similarly, on similar notes, E-Sanjeevani is a telemedicine platform launched by the Ministry of Health and Family Welfare in 2020. It enables remote consultations between patients and doctors, particularly in rural and remote areas where access to healthcare is limited. E-Sanjeevani has witnessed significant adoption during the COVID-19 pandemic, highlighting the potential of telemedicine to bridge the gap in healthcare access.

While the challenges facing India's healthcare system are immense, the positive developments and promising initiatives offer a ray of hope for the future. The advances in medical technology, successful public health campaigns, dedication of healthcare workers, and government initiatives such as Ayushman Bharat, NDHM, and E-Sanjeevani demonstrate the potential for progress.

However, realizing this potential will require sustained commitment, investment, and collaboration between the government, healthcare providers, and civil society along with private players in the market. It will also require addressing the systemic issues of corruption, inefficiency, and poor governance that continue to plague the system.

By building on these positive developments and addressing the root causes of the healthcare crisis, India can create a healthcare system that is accessible, affordable, and equitable for all its citizens. The journey may be long and challenging, but the destination - a healthy and prosperous India - is worth striving for.

A Tale of Two Cities

The morning sun cast long shadows across the bustling ward, its rays filtering through the grime-streaked windows and illuminating the faces of the patients. Dr. Madhav, his white coat starched and crisp, moved with quiet purpose through the throng, his presence a beacon of hope in the sea of suffering. It was almost as if he was making up for all the unpainted and chipped walls with his peaceful aura. Amidst cries and screams, his composure and clarity clearly showed his experience.

At the gate of the general ward, a young and tired face appeared waiting for him with a heavy file.

"Busy day, Nakul?"

"Didn't sleep at all, sir," the young man complained, "I was covering for Naina's shift last night. Sudden overflow came in last night. A bus trampled and fell off the flyover. Spent some time covering that, after some relief, finally, the second I sat to drink some water, an unidentifiable person was brought in. Burns, cuts, everything. No ID."

"Busy day it is." asserted Dr. Madhav.

His morning rounds once had a bunch of residents running around him, getting updates, handling patients. But, that was a different lifetime. Those were different struggles. As if a different lifetime altogether.

He paused beside an elderly woman, her face etched with worry, and gently examined the swollen bandage on her leg." The infection is clearing up nicely, Nakul," he reassured her with a warm smile and then instructed her calmly, "Keep the dressing clean and dry, and you'll be back on your feet in no time."

Next, he moved on to a young boy, his arm encased in a plaster cast. "How's that cricket injury healing, Arjun?" he asked, his voice laced with playful concern. The boy grinned, flexing his fingers tentatively. "Almost as good as new! Thanks to you!"

Madhav's heart swelled with a sense of fulfillment. This was why he had returned to India, to make a difference in the lives of those who needed it most. The elderly woman can now soon get back to work to support her children. And the child can finally get back to his normal life, even if it's going from house to house collecting garbage, of course, only after he is done from school, or on a leave. But the joy was fleeting as always, quickly replaced by a sobering reality as he approached the far corner of the ward.

There, amidst the tangle of beds and bodies, lay Parth, his face a horrifying testament to the cruelty of fate. He shared a bed with another patient, a middle-aged man whose leg was suspended in traction, his groans of pain adding to the ward's symphony of suffering.

Madhav's mind flashed back to a similar case he had encountered years ago in the US. A young woman, her face ravaged by a fire, had been rushed to his hospital. The best burn specialists, state-of-the-art equipment, and a dedicated team had worked tirelessly to reconstruct her features, to give her back her life. He then recalled his time in private Indian hospitals, where at least a private room and specialized care were available,even if the resources paled in comparison to those in the West.

It was the best of times, it was the worst of times, it was the age of wisdom, it was the age of foolishness, it was the epoch of belief, it was the epoch of incredulity, it was the season of Light, it was the season of Darkness, it was the spring of hope, it was the winter of despair, we had everything before us, we had nothing before us, we were all going direct to Heaven, we were all going direct the other way — in short, the period was so far like the present period, that some of its noisiest authorities insisted on its being received, for good or for evil, in the superlative degree of comparison only.

The above iconic words, penned by Charles Dickens in his timeless novel, resonate with a chilling familiarity when applied to the landscape of healthcare in India today. It is a tale of two cities, a stark dichotomy between the privileged and the underserved, where the promise of healing and well-being coexists with the harsh realities of disparity and neglect.

On one side of this divide stands the gleaming citadel of private healthcare, a realm where cutting-edge technology, personalized care, and world-class facilities converge to create an oasis of comfort and healing. Here, patients are greeted with smiles, ushered into plush waiting areas, and guided through a seamless admission process. The outpatient departments (OPDs) are meticulously organized, with shorter waiting times and dedicated staff to cater to every need. The wards, spacious and well-equipped, offer a serene environment conducive to recovery.

In stark contrast, the public healthcare system, burdened by a multitude of challenges, often resembles a scene from a dystopian novel. Overcrowded wards, endless queues, and a perpetual shortage of essential medicines and equipment paint a picture of a system struggling to cope with the demands of a vast and diverse population. The admission process itself is a harrowing ordeal, a testament to the system's inadequacies and the immense challenges faced by those seeking care.

This stark contrast, a reflection of deep-seated socioeconomic inequalities, paints a grim picture of a nation grappling with the challenge of providing equitable healthcare to its citizens. It is a tale of two realities, where the quality of care one receives is often determined by their ability to pay, a reality that is both unjust and unsustainable.

In the chapters that follow, we will navigate the labyrinthine world of public and private healthcare, examining the disparities in access and affordability, the ethical dilemmas faced by healthcare professionals, and the urgent need for systemic reforms.

India's healthcare system mirrors the nation's multifaceted nature, a tapestry woven with threads of both opulence and austerity. It is a tale of two cities, a stark dichotomy between the privileged and the underserved. On one side stands the gleaming citadel of private healthcare, a sanctuary of cutting-edge technology, personalized care, and world-class facilities. On the other side lies the overburdened and under-resourced public healthcare system, a labyrinthine world of overcrowded wards, endless queues, and a perpetual shortage of essential medicines and equipment. This stark contrast, a reflection of deep-seated socioeconomic inequalities, paints a grim picture of a nation grappling with the challenge of providing equitable healthcare to its citizens.

Stepping into a private hospital in India is akin to entering a different world, a realm where the anxieties and uncertainties of illness are met with a reassuring embrace of comfort and care. The gleaming facades, the pristine interiors, the hushed tones of the staff - all conspire to create an atmosphere of tranquility and hope.

The patient experience in private healthcare is meticulously curated, starting from the moment they step through the doors. A warm smile greets them, a gesture that speaks volumes in a time of vulnerability. Plush waiting areas, adorned with comfortable seating, soothing music, and perhaps even a complimentary beverage, offer a respite from the harsh realities of the outside world. The admission process is seamless, with dedicated staff members guiding patients through the paperwork and formalities, ensuring a hassle-free experience.

The outpatient departments (OPDs) are a model of efficiency, with shorter waiting times and a well-organized system that minimizes delays and frustrations. Patients are assigned specific time slots, ensuring that their valuable time is not wasted in endless queues. Dedicated staff members are on hand to assist with registration, provide information, and guide patients to the appropriate departments. The environment is clean, well-lit, and equipped with modern amenities, creating a sense of order and professionalism.

The wards, spacious and well-equipped, offer a serene and comfortable environment conducive to healing. Private rooms, equipped with modern amenities and attentive staff, provide patients with the privacy and dignity they deserve. The doctor-to-patient ratio is favorable, allowing for more comprehensive consultations and personalized treatment plans. The nursing staff, highly trained and well-compensated, provides round-the-clock care, ensuring that every patient's needs are met with compassion and expertise.

The pharmacies in private hospitals are a testament to the abundance of resources. They are well-stocked with a wide range of medications, including the latest patented drugs, ensuring that patients have access to the most advanced treatments available. The focus is on providing not just medical treatment, but a holistic healing experience that addresses the physical, emotional, and psychological needs of the patient.

In this realm of privilege, the patient is king. Every aspect of their care is meticulously managed, from the initial consultation to the final discharge, ensuring a smooth and stress-free journey towards recovery. The emphasis is on providing not just treatment but also a sense of empowerment, where patients are actively involved in their healthcare decisions and their voices are heard.

However, this idyllic picture of private healthcare is accessible only to a privileged few. The high cost of treatment,often running into lakhs of rupees, places it beyond the reach of the vast majority of the population. This creates a stark divide, where the quality of healthcare one receives is often determined by their ability to pay, a reality that is both unjust and unsustainable.

In stark contrast to the oasis of private care lies the labyrinthine world of public healthcare, a stark and often overwhelming reality for the majority of India's population. Here, the picture is one of scarcity and struggle, where the sheer volume of patients seeking care often overwhelms the limited resources and infrastructure.

The admission process in public hospitals can be a daunting ordeal. Long queues snake through crowded corridors, patients and their families jostling for space and vying for attention. The air is thick with a mixture of anxiety, frustration,and resignation. The bureaucratic hurdles, the endless forms to fill, and the lack of clear information can be overwhelming, particularly for those who are already grappling with the burden of illness. The wait for a simple consultation can stretch into hours, and the process of getting admitted can be even more arduous.

The wards, often cramped and poorly ventilated, offer little respite from the suffering. Beds are crammed together,privacy is a luxury, and the constant din of human misery creates a stressful environment that can hinder the healing process. The doctor-to-patient ratio is alarmingly high, with overworked physicians struggling to provide adequate care to the overwhelming number of patients. The nursing staff, though dedicated and compassionate, is often stretched thin, their efforts hampered by a lack of resources and support.

The pharmacies in public hospitals, often understocked and underfunded, reflect the scarcity that permeates the system.Patients are frequently forced to purchase medications from outside pharmacies, adding to their financial burden. The lack of access to essential drugs and the high cost of treatment can have devastating consequences, leading to delayed or inadequate care and, in some cases, even preventable deaths.

This stark dichotomy between private and public healthcare in India is a reflection of the deep-seated socioeconomic inequalities that plague the nation. While the privileged few can access a world of comfort and efficiency, the vast majority are left to navigate a system that is often chaotic, impersonal, and unresponsive to their needs.

The consequences of this inequality are far-reaching. Studies have shown that individuals from lower socioeconomic backgrounds have higher rates of mortality and morbidity, limited access to preventive care, and delayed diagnosis and treatment of chronic diseases. The financial burden of healthcare often pushes them deeper into poverty, creating a vicious cycle that is difficult to break.

The tale of two cities in Indian healthcare is a story of privilege and neglect, a reflection of a society where access to quality care is often determined by one's ability to pay. It is a challenge that demands urgent attention and a concerted effort from all stakeholders to create a more equitable and accessible healthcare system for all.

The government must prioritize the strengthening of the public healthcare system, investing in infrastructure, human resources, and technology. It must also implement policies that promote greater equity and accessibility, such as universal health coverage and price controls on essential medications.

The private sector, too, has a crucial role to play. It must recognize its social responsibility and actively contribute to the development of affordable and accessible healthcare solutions. This can be achieved through collaborations with the public sector, investment in research and development, and the provision of pro-bono services and community outreach programs.

Ultimately, the goal is to create a healthcare system that truly serves the needs of all, regardless of their socioeconomic status. It is a journey towards a future where quality healthcare is not a privilege but a fundamental right for every Indian citizen.

The very first step in seeking medical care, the admission process, unveils a stark contrast between the privileged world of private healthcare and the often chaotic reality of the public sector. In private hospitals, patients are greeted with a warm smile, a comforting gesture that eases their anxieties. They are ushered into plush waiting areas, adorned with comfortable seating, soothing music, and perhaps even a complimentary cup of tea. The admission process itself is streamlined and efficient, with dedicated staff members guiding patients through the paperwork and formalities,ensuring a seamless and stress-free experience.

The outpatient departments (OPDs), the gateway to medical care for millions of Indians, further highlight this disparity.In private hospitals, OPDs are typically well-organized and efficiently managed. Patients are assigned specific time slots, minimizing waiting times and ensuring a smooth flow of patients. Dedicated staff members are on hand to assist with registration, provide information, and guide patients to the appropriate departments. The environment is generally clean and comfortable, with ample seating and amenities to cater to the needs of patients and their families.

In stark contrast to the serene oasis of private healthcare, the public healthcare system in India often resembles a scene from a dystopian novel, a labyrinthine world where patients navigate a maze of overcrowded corridors, bureaucratic hurdles, and a perpetual sense of despair. The admission process itself is a harrowing ordeal, a stark testament to the system's inadequacies and the immense challenges faced by those seeking care.

Long queues snake through the dimly lit corridors, a sea of humanity united by their shared vulnerability and desperation. Patients, their faces etched with anxiety and pain, jostle for space, their voices rising in a cacophony of pleas and complaints. The air hangs heavy with the mingled scents of sweat, antiseptic, and unwashed bodies, a pungent reminder of the overcrowding and neglect that permeate the system. The bureaucratic machinery grinds slowly,its gears clogged with endless forms, missing documents, and a lack of clear information. For those already grappling with the burden of illness, this labyrinthine process can be overwhelming, a cruel obstacle course that stands between them and the care they desperately need.

A 2019 study revealed the grim reality of this ordeal, with the average waiting time for a consultation in a public hospital OPD in India exceeding two hours. Some patients reported waits of up to six hours or more, their hopes dwindling with each passing minute. This agonizing wait, often endured in cramped and uncomfortable conditions, can exacerbate existing health conditions and create a breeding ground for frustration and despair.

The outpatient departments (OPDs), the gateway to medical care for millions of Indians, further highlight this disparity.In private hospitals, OPDs are typically well-organized and efficiently managed, with patients assigned specific time slots and dedicated staff members to guide them through the process. The environment is clean and comfortable,offering a sense of dignity and respect to those seeking care.

In the heart of India's public healthcare system lies a stark reality: the outpatient departments (OPDs), the gateway to medical care for millions, are often scenes of overwhelming chaos and overcrowding. The sheer volume of patients seeking care can be staggering, with some hospitals reporting OPD attendance exceeding their capacity by a mind-boggling 200-300%. The waiting areas, once designed to provide a space for patients to rest and gather their thoughts before consultations, are transformed into bustling marketplaces, teeming with humanity and echoing with a symphony of coughs, groans, and anxious whispers.

The sheer density of people within these confined spaces is palpable. Patients and their families, often hailing from distant villages and towns, jostle for a sliver of space on hard benches or even the floor, their belongings piled around them. The air hangs heavy with the mingled scents of sweat, antiseptic, and illness, a potent reminder of the collective suffering that permeates the space. The heat, particularly during the sweltering summer months, adds another layer of discomfort, turning the waiting areas into veritable furnaces where patience and resilience are tested to their limits.

The lack of privacy is another striking feature of these overcrowded OPDs. Intimate conversations about medical histories and symptoms are often conducted in hushed tones, amidst the din of surrounding conversations and the occasional wails of children. The sense of vulnerability and exposure is amplified by the constant stream of people passing by, their curious glances adding to the patients' anxieties.

The overworked staff, their faces etched with exhaustion and a hint of resignation, struggle to maintain order and provide even a modicum of comfort to the throngs of patients. The registration counters are besieged by anxious faces,each vying for attention and a chance to be seen by a doctor. The queues for consultations snake through the corridors,their length a testament to the sheer demand for medical care.

The noise level in these OPDs is often deafening. The cacophony of voices, the cries of children, the beeping of medical equipment, and the occasional announcements over the crackling public address system create a constant hum that can be both disorienting and distressing. For patients already grappling with the burden of illness, this sensory overload can be overwhelming, exacerbating their anxieties and hindering their ability to communicate effectively with healthcare providers.

Amidst this chaos, patients often feel reduced to mere numbers in a system struggling to cope with the overwhelming demand. The impersonal nature of the interactions, the hurried consultations, and the lack of continuity of care can leave patients feeling neglected and dehumanized. The focus on efficiency, driven by the sheer volume of patients,often overshadows the need for empathy and compassion, leaving patients feeling like cogs in a machine rather than individuals in need of care.

The impact of overcrowding on the quality of care in public hospitals is undeniable. Overworked and understaffed medical personnel, struggling to keep up with the relentless flow of patients, are often forced to make quick decisions and compromises that can impact patient outcomes. The lack of adequate time for thorough consultations, the pressure to move patients through the system quickly, and the limited availability of resources can all contribute to misdiagnosis,delayed treatment, and suboptimal care.

Moreover, the psychological toll of overcrowding on patients cannot be ignored. The long waits, the lack of privacy, the constant noise and commotion can all contribute to increased anxiety, stress, and a sense of helplessness. This can negatively impact patients' overall well-being and their ability to cope with their illnesses.

The overcrowded OPDs in public hospitals are a stark reminder of the challenges facing the Indian healthcare system.They are a testament to the immense demand for medical care, the limited resources available, and the urgent need for systemic reforms to ensure that every citizen has access to quality healthcare. Addressing this issue will require a multi-pronged approach that includes increasing investment in healthcare infrastructure, expanding the healthcare workforce,and implementing innovative solutions to improve efficiency and accessibility.

It is a challenge that demands the collective efforts of policymakers, healthcare professionals, and the community at large. By working together, we can create a healthcare system that is not only efficient but also compassionate, one that prioritizes the dignity and well-being of every patient, regardless of their socioeconomic status. Only then can we truly fulfill the promise of healthcare as a fundamental right for all.

The understaffed and overworked medical personnel, the true heroes of the public healthcare system, are often stretched to their limits, their efforts hampered by a lack of resources and infrastructure. A 2022 report by the National Health Systems Resource Centre revealed that over 50% of public hospitals in India operate with less than 70% of their sanctioned staff strength. This means that doctors, nurses, and other healthcare professionals are often forced to work long hours, juggling multiple responsibilities, and making difficult decisions about prioritizing care. The physical and emotional toll of this relentless workload is immense, leading to burnout, compassion fatigue, and a decline in the quality of care.

Patients, many of whom have traveled long distances from remote villages and towns, often arrive at public hospitals with a flicker of hope in their eyes, only to be met with a system that seems indifferent to their suffering. The long waits, the impersonal interactions, the lack of clear communication - it all contributes to a sense of frustration, neglect,and a loss of faith in the system. For those already grappling with the burden of illness, this experience can be devastating, eroding their dignity and leaving them feeling like mere cogs in a broken machine.

Nurses stand as pillars of compassion and care, their presence a beacon of hope in the often tumultuous world of hospitals and clinics. They are the silent sentinels of the night, the gentle hands that soothe and comfort, the vigilant eyes that monitor every fluctuation of a patient's condition. Their tireless dedication and skilled hands are instrumental in ensuring the well-being of those under their care, their unwavering commitment to their calling a testament to the profound impact they have on countless lives.

In the realm of private healthcare, nurses often find themselves in an environment that fosters their professional growth and empowers them to provide optimal patient care. They receive extensive training, equipping them with the latest medical knowledge and techniques to handle a wide array of conditions. The patient-to-nurse ratio is typically lower,allowing for more personalized attention and a deeper connection with each individual. They are also equipped with state-of-the-art technology and resources, enabling them to deliver efficient and effective care. This combination of factors creates an environment where nurses can truly flourish, their compassion and expertise translating into a holistic approach to patient care that prioritizes both physical and emotional well-being.

However, the reality in public hospitals paints a starkly different picture. The nursing profession in India, despite its critical importance, grapples with a myriad of challenges that often overshadow their invaluable contributions. The sheer volume of patients, coupled with a chronic shortage of nursing staff, creates a demanding and often overwhelming work environment. Nurses are constantly juggling multiple responsibilities, from administering medications and monitoring vital signs to providing emotional support and educating patients about their conditions.The physical and emotional toll of this relentless workload is immense, leading to burnout, compassion fatigue, and a sense of helplessness among the nursing staff.

The lack of adequate resources further exacerbates the challenges faced by nurses in public hospitals. From basic medical supplies like gloves and syringes to advanced equipment like ventilators and dialysis machines, shortages are a common occurrence. This forces nurses to make difficult choices, prioritize care based on limited resources, and sometimes even improvise solutions to meet the needs of their patients. The constant struggle to provide adequate care in the face of such constraints can be demoralizing and can lead to a sense of disillusionment among even the most dedicated nurses.

Despite these challenges, nurses in public hospitals continue to serve with unwavering dedication, their compassion shining through even in the darkest of times. They are the ones who hold the hands of the dying, offering comfort and solace in their final moments. They are the ones who celebrate the small victories of recovery, their smiles a beacon of hope for patients and their families. They are the ones who educate patients about their conditions, empowering them to take control of their health and make informed decisions.

The value of nurses in the healthcare system cannot be overstated. They are the bridge between patients and doctors,the advocates for those who cannot speak for themselves, the caregivers who provide comfort and support when it is needed most. Their tireless efforts, their unwavering compassion, and their skilled hands are instrumental in ensuring the well-being of countless individuals.

It is time to recognize the invaluable contributions of nurses, to address their challenges, and to create a work environment that fosters their growth and well-being. By investing in their training, providing adequate resources, and offering fair compensation and recognition, we can empower nurses to fulfill their potential and ensure that every patient, regardless of their socioeconomic status, receives the compassionate and skilled care they deserve.

In the realm of private healthcare, nurses often find themselves in an environment conducive to optimal patient care.They undergo rigorous training, equipping them with the latest medical knowledge and techniques to handle a wide array of conditions. The patient-to-nurse ratio is typically lower, with some private hospitals boasting a 1:3 or even 1:2 ratio, allowing for more personalized attention and a deeper connection with each individual. Moreover, they are equipped with the latest technology and resources, enabling them to provide efficient and effective care. This combination of factors fosters an environment where nurses can truly flourish, their compassion and expertise translating into a holistic approach to patient care that prioritizes both physical and emotional well-being.

However, the reality in public hospitals is a stark departure from this ideal. The sheer volume of patients, coupled with a chronic shortage of nursing staff, creates a demanding and often overwhelming work environment. The World Health Organization recommends a nurse-to-patient ratio of 1:430, but in India, this ratio can be as high as 1:1100 in some public hospitals. Nurses are constantly juggling multiple responsibilities, racing against the clock to administer medications, monitor vital signs, and provide basic care to a seemingly endless stream of patients. The physical and emotional toll of this relentless workload is immense, with studies indicating that over 70% of nurses in public hospitals experience burnout and compassion fatigue.

The lack of adequate resources further exacerbates the challenges faced by nurses in public hospitals. From basic medical supplies like gloves and syringes to advanced equipment like ventilators and dialysis machines, shortages are a common occurrence. A 2020 survey revealed that over 60% of public hospitals in India reported shortages of essential medical supplies, forcing nurses to make difficult choices, prioritize care based on limited resources, and sometimes even improvise solutions to meet the needs of their patients. The constant struggle to provide adequate care in the face of such constraints can be demoralizing and can lead to a sense of disillusionment among even the most dedicated nurses.

The financial strain on nurses in the public sector adds another layer of complexity to their already challenging circumstances. Despite their critical role in the healthcare system, nurses in public hospitals are often woefully underpaid. Their salaries, which can be as low as ₹10,000-₹15,000 per month for entry-level positions, stand in stark contrast to the lucrative compensation packages offered by private hospitals. This financial insecurity, coupled with the demanding work environment and lack of recognition, can lead to a high turnover rate, further exacerbating the nursing shortage and perpetuating the cycle of understaffing and burnout.

The stories of these nurses, their voices often drowned out by the clamor of overcrowded wards and the relentless demands of their profession, are a testament to their resilience and unwavering dedication. They are the ones who work tirelessly, often beyond their scheduled hours, to ensure that their patients receive the best possible care, even in the face of overwhelming odds. They are the ones who hold the hands of the dying, who offer a comforting word to the anxious, who celebrate the small victories of recovery. Their compassion, even in the face of adversity, is a beacon of hope in a system that is often plagued by despair.

The disparity in nursing care between the private and public sectors is a reflection of the broader inequalities that permeate the Indian healthcare landscape. It is a call to action, a reminder that the true strength of any healthcare system lies in its human capital. By investing in the training, well-being, and recognition of nurses, we can not only improve the quality of care but also create a more just and equitable healthcare system for all. It is time to bridge the gap between the two worlds of nursing, to ensure that every patient, regardless of their socioeconomic status, receives the compassionate and skilled care they deserve.

Just look at the irony that, India, often hailed as the "pharmacy of the world," is a global leader in the production and export of generic drugs, providing affordable medications to millions across the globe. However, this narrative of success masks a stark reality within the country itself: the high cost of patented medications remains a formidable barrier for countless Indian patients, creating a healthcare landscape where the price of life itself is often beyond the reach of the common man.

The absence of effective price regulation has allowed some pharmaceutical companies to exploit their monopoly on patented drugs, charging exorbitant prices that are simply unaffordable for the majority of the population. This is particularly evident in the case of life-saving medications for chronic and debilitating diseases such as cancer,HIV/AIDS, and hepatitis C.

A 2022 study by the Public Health Foundation of India revealed the shocking disparity between drug prices and the average Indian's income. The average cost of a month's supply of cancer medication can range from ₹20,000 to a staggering ₹1,00,000. This is a cruel irony in a country where the average monthly income hovers around ₹18,000.Similarly, before the introduction of generic versions, the cost of a full course of patented Hepatitis C drugs was as high as ₹70,000, a price tag that condemned millions of infected Indians to a life of suffering and premature death.

The consequences of this affordability crisis are nothing short of devastating. Millions of Indians are forced to make agonizing choices, delaying or even abandoning treatment as they grapple with the impossible dilemma of choosing between financial ruin and their health. The lack of access to essential medications not only impacts individual lives but also has a ripple effect on families and communities, perpetuating a cycle of poverty and ill-health.

The World Bank, in a 2019 report, estimated that out-of-pocket expenditure on healthcare pushes over 55 million Indians into poverty each year. This staggering figure underscores the catastrophic impact of high drug prices on vulnerable populations. Families are forced to sell their assets, borrow money at exorbitant interest rates, or even resort to crowdfunding to afford life-saving medications. The emotional and psychological toll of this financial burden is immeasurable, adding to the already immense suffering caused by the disease itself.

The lack of robust regulatory oversight further exacerbates the problem of unaffordable medications. While the Indian government has taken steps to regulate drug prices through the National Pharmaceutical Pricing Authority (NPPA), the system remains riddled with loopholes and inconsistencies. The process of price fixation is often shrouded in secrecy,with limited transparency and public participation. This creates an environment where powerful pharmaceutical companies can exert undue influence, lobbying for favorable pricing decisions that prioritize their profits over the needs of patients.

Moreover, the enforcement of price controls is often lax, allowing companies to circumvent regulations and charge exorbitant prices for their products. A 2021 study by the Centre for Science and Environment revealed a disturbing trend: over 40% of essential medicines were being sold at prices higher than the ceiling price fixed by the NPPA. This widespread non-compliance highlights the urgent need for stricter enforcement mechanisms and greater accountability within the pharmaceutical sector.

The crisis of affordability in the Indian pharmaceutical industry is a complex issue with no easy solutions. It demands a multi-pronged approach that involves not only stricter price controls and regulatory oversight but also a fundamental shift in the industry's mindset towards prioritizing patient welfare over profit motives.

The government must take a proactive role in ensuring that essential medications are accessible and affordable to all.This includes strengthening the NPPA, making the price fixation process more transparent and inclusive, and implementing stricter penalties for non-compliance. The government should also explore innovative financing mechanisms, such as bulk procurement and compulsory licensing, to reduce the cost of essential drugs.

The pharmaceutical industry, too, has a crucial role to play. It must recognize its social responsibility and actively contribute to making medications more affordable. This could involve voluntary price reductions, tiered pricing models for different socioeconomic groups, and greater investment in research and development for affordable healthcare solutions.

Furthermore, there is a need for greater awareness and advocacy around the issue of drug affordability. Civil society organizations, patient advocacy groups, and the media must play a proactive role in highlighting the plight of patients struggling to afford life-saving medications. They must also hold the government and the pharmaceutical industry accountable for their actions, demanding greater transparency, accountability, and a commitment to patient welfare.

This dire situation has led to a growing chorus of voices demanding greater affordability and accessibility of essential medications. Patient advocacy groups, civil society organizations, and even some within the medical community have been vocal in their criticism of the current system, calling for stricter price controls, greater transparency in drug pricing, and increased government intervention to ensure that life-saving medications are within the reach of all.

In the face of daunting healthcare challenges, the Indian government has embarked on a series of ambitious initiatives aimed at improving access to care for the poor and marginalized. These schemes, often heralded as beacons of hope,seek to bridge the gap between the haves and have-nots, ensuring that quality healthcare is not a privilege but a fundamental right for all citizens.

In the face of India's complex healthcare landscape, where stark disparities and systemic inadequacies cast a long shadow over the nation's well-being, the government has embarked on a series of ambitious initiatives aimed at improving access to care for the poor and marginalized. Among these, the Ayushman Bharat Pradhan Mantri Jan Arogya Yojana (AB-PMJAY), launched in 2018, stands out as a beacon of hope, a bold attempt to provide a safety net for those most vulnerable to the financial burdens of healthcare.

Dubbed as the world's largest health insurance scheme, AB-PMJAY aims to provide health coverage of up to ₹5 lakhs per family per year for secondary and tertiary care hospitalization to over 500 million beneficiaries, representing the bottom 40% of the Indian population. This ambitious scheme, with its promise of cashless hospitalization and a wide network of empaneled hospitals, has the potential to revolutionize healthcare access for millions, offering financial protection against catastrophic health expenditures that can push families into poverty.

AB-PMJAY is not the only initiative undertaken by the government to address the healthcare needs of its citizens. The Rashtriya Swasthya Bima Yojana (RSBY), launched in 2008, provides health insurance coverage to Below Poverty Line (BPL) families, offering them financial protection against hospitalization expenses. The Janani Suraksha Yojana (JSY), another flagship program, incentivizes institutional deliveries to reduce maternal and infant mortality rates, a critical step towards improving maternal and child health outcomes. These schemes, along with various state-level initiatives, represent a concerted effort by the government to bridge the healthcare gap and ensure that every citizen has access to essential medical services.

However, the path to universal health coverage is fraught with challenges. The implementation of these schemes has been hampered by a multitude of factors, including inadequate funding, bureaucratic hurdles, and a lack of awareness among the target population. Many eligible beneficiaries remain unaware of the benefits they are entitled to, while others struggle to navigate the complex enrollment and claims processes. The lack of adequate infrastructure and trained personnel in many public healthcare facilities further limits the reach and impact of these schemes.

The low utilization rate of AB-PMJAY, with only 30% of eligible beneficiaries availing themselves of the scheme's benefits as of 2021, highlights the challenges in reaching the target population and ensuring that they are aware of and able to access the benefits.

The low utilization rate of AB-PMJAY, a stark reality that belies its ambitious goals, can be attributed to several factors that hinder its reach and effectiveness. These barriers, ranging from lack of awareness to systemic inadequacies, create a chasm between the promise of the scheme and its actual implementation, leaving millions of eligible beneficiaries in the lurch.

One of the most significant barriers to the success of AB-PMJAY is the lack of awareness among the target population,particularly those residing in rural areas and marginalized communities. Despite the government's efforts to publicize the scheme through various channels, including television, radio, and print media, many eligible beneficiaries remain unaware of its existence or its benefits. This is partly due to limited outreach and communication efforts, particularly in remote and underserved areas where access to information is often restricted. The lack of awareness translates into missed opportunities for healthcare, as individuals who could potentially benefit from the scheme remain unaware of their entitlements.

The enrollment and claims processes under AB-PMJAY, while designed to ensure transparency and accountability, can often be cumbersome and time-consuming. The requirement for extensive documentation, including proof of identity,address, and income, can be a major hurdle for those who lack access to official records or have limited literacy skills.Moreover, the process often involves multiple visits to government offices, which can be a daunting task for those who are already grappling with health issues and financial constraints. This bureaucratic maze, coupled with a lack of clear and easily accessible information, can deter many eligible beneficiaries from enrolling in the scheme or utilizing its benefits.

The lack of adequate infrastructure and trained personnel in many public healthcare facilities further limits the reach and impact of AB-PMJAY. While the scheme promises cashless hospitalization at a network of empaneled hospitals,the reality on the ground is often different. Many public hospitals, particularly in rural areas, lack the necessary infrastructure, equipment, and specialized medical professionals to provide the quality of care promised under the scheme. This can lead to delays in treatment, complications, and even denial of claims, leaving patients frustrated and disillusioned. The shortage of trained personnel, including doctors, nurses, and administrative staff, further exacerbates the problem, creating bottlenecks in the system and hindering the efficient delivery of care.

A general lack of trust in government schemes, fueled by past experiences of corruption, inefficiency, and broken promises, also contributes to the low utilization rate of AB-PMJAY. Many people, particularly those from marginalized communities, are skeptical about the effectiveness and transparency of the scheme, fearing that it might be another empty promise or a tool for political gain. This trust deficit can lead to hesitancy in enrolling in the scheme and utilizing its benefits, even when they are desperately needed.

Addressing these challenges requires a multi-pronged approach that focuses on improving awareness, streamlining processes, strengthening infrastructure, and building trust. The government must invest in robust outreach and communication campaigns to educate the target population about the benefits of the scheme and how to access them.The enrollment and claims processes must be simplified and made more user-friendly, leveraging technology to reduce bureaucratic hurdles and improve efficiency.

Furthermore, significant investments are needed to strengthen the public healthcare infrastructure, particularly in rural areas. This includes building new hospitals and clinics, upgrading existing facilities, and ensuring adequate staffing and supplies. Training and capacity building of healthcare professionals, particularly at the primary and secondary levels, is also crucial to ensure the effective implementation of the scheme.

Building trust in government schemes is a long-term process that requires transparency, accountability, and consistent delivery of services. The government must ensure that the scheme is implemented in a fair and equitable manner, with clear guidelines and grievance redressal mechanisms in place.

The success of AB-PMJAY and other government schemes hinges on addressing these challenges and ensuring that the benefits reach those who need them the most. It is a journey that demands the collective efforts of policymakers,healthcare professionals, civil society organizations, and the community at large. By working together, we can create a healthcare system that is truly inclusive, equitable, and accessible to all, fulfilling the promise of a healthier and happier India.

Moreover, the financial sustainability of these schemes remains a concern. The allocation of funds for healthcare in the national budget remains woefully inadequate, and the increasing burden of chronic diseases and lifestyle-related illnesses poses a significant challenge to the long-term viability of these schemes.

While government schemes, like flickering candles in a storm, offer a glimmer of hope in the relentless fight for healthcare equity, their true potential remains shrouded in the shadows of systemic challenges that impede their implementation. It is a stark reality that the path to a just and equitable healthcare system is not paved with good intentions alone; it demands a multi-pronged approach that tackles the root causes of inequality and empowers every citizen to access the care they deserve.

In a nation where out-of-pocket expenditure accounts for a staggering 70% of healthcare costs, health insurance emerges as a critical safety net, shielding individuals and families from the financial devastation of unexpected illness or injury. However, the landscape of health insurance in India is marred by significant challenges, including a lack of coverage in rural areas and the inadequacies of existing insurance schemes. This article delves into the complexities of health insurance in India, examining its reach, limitations, and the urgent need for comprehensive reform.

The penetration of health insurance in India remains woefully low, with only around 41% of the population covered as of 2021. This leaves a vast majority of Indians, particularly those in rural areas and from lower socioeconomic backgrounds,vulnerable to the financial burden of healthcare expenses.

The disparity in health insurance coverage between urban and rural areas is stark. While urban areas have witnessed a gradual increase in health insurance penetration, driven by rising awareness and the availability of private insurance schemes, rural areas continue to lag behind. The lack of awareness, limited access to insurance providers, and the perception of health insurance as a luxury rather than a necessity contribute to this divide.

The affordability of health insurance is a major barrier for many Indians, particularly those from lower socioeconomic backgrounds. The high premiums and complex terms and conditions of many private insurance schemes make them inaccessible to the poor and vulnerable. This creates a situation where those who need health insurance the most are often the least likely to have it.

While the Indian government has launched several health insurance schemes, including the flagship Ayushman Bharat program, these initiatives face challenges in terms of coverage, adequacy, and implementation.

Many existing health insurance schemes offer limited coverage, excluding certain pre-existing conditions, chronic illnesses, and high-cost treatments. This leaves patients with significant out-of-pocket expenses, defeating the purpose of insurance as a financial safety net. The sum insured under many health insurance schemes is often insufficient to cover the rising cost of healthcare,particularly for critical illnesses and prolonged hospital stays. This forces patients to bear a substantial portion of the expenses, leading to financial hardship. The implementation of health insurance schemes in India is often marred by challenges such as lack of awareness,cumbersome claim processes, and delays in reimbursement. This creates frustration and distrust among beneficiaries,undermining the effectiveness of these schemes.

I remember reading in a newspaper about a farmer from a remote village in Rajasthan, was diagnosed with a heart condition requiring surgery. Despite being enrolled in a government health insurance scheme, the limited coverage and delays in reimbursement forced him to sell his land to pay for the surgery. This left him and his family in dire financial straits, highlighting the limitations of existing insurance schemes in protecting the vulnerable from catastrophic health expenditures.

Another such case I heard of was of a domestic worker in Mumbai, who developed complications during childbirth. While she had a private health insurance policy, the exclusions and sub-limits in her policy meant that she had to pay a significant portion of the hospital bill. This unexpected expense pushed her into debt, demonstrating the inadequacy of many private insurance schemes in providing comprehensive coverage.

Addressing the challenges in India's health insurance landscape requires a multi-pronged approach that focuses on expanding coverage, improving the adequacy of existing schemes, and streamlining implementation.

Increasing the penetration of health insurance, particularly in rural areas and among the poor and vulnerable, is crucial.This can be achieved through a combination of government-sponsored schemes, community-based health insurance models, and innovative micro-insurance products. Existing health insurance schemes need to be revamped to provide more comprehensive coverage, including pre-existing conditions, chronic illnesses, and high-cost treatments. Increasing the sum insured and reducing out-of-pocket expenses are also essential to ensure that insurance truly acts as a financial safety net. Simplifying the enrollment and claim processes, leveraging technology for faster and more efficient claim settlements, and strengthening grievance redressal mechanisms are crucial for improving the implementation of health insurance schemes. Creating awareness about the importance of health insurance and educating people about the available schemes and their benefits is essential to increase enrollment and utilization.

But here's the reality: This journey towards a healthier India necessitates a paradigm shift, a move away from reactive treatment towards proactive prevention. It calls for a renewed focus on public health initiatives, from robust immunization programs and disease surveillance to health education and awareness campaigns that empower individuals to take charge of their well-being. It is a clarion call for greater investment in healthcare infrastructure, particularly in underserved areas, ensuring that every citizen, regardless of their geographical location, has access to quality medical facilities and trained personnel.

The bureaucratic maze that often ensnares beneficiaries of government schemes must be dismantled, replaced by streamlined processes that are accessible, transparent, and user-friendly. Leveraging technology, simplifying documentation requirements, and establishing clear communication channels can go a long way in ensuring that the benefits of these schemes reach those who need them the most.

Building trust in government initiatives is a long and arduous process, but it is essential for their success. Transparency,accountability, and consistent delivery of services are key to fostering confidence and encouraging greater participation.The government must work tirelessly to dispel the skepticism that often surrounds such schemes, demonstrating their commitment to serving the people and upholding the principles of equity and justice.

As we stand at this critical juncture, let us not be deterred by the challenges that lie ahead. Let us draw inspiration from the countless individuals who have fought for a more just and equitable healthcare system, their voices echoing through the corridors of time. Let us work together, with unwavering dedication and a shared vision, to create a healthcare landscape where the promise of healing and well-being is not a distant dream but a tangible reality for all.

Brave New World

A couple of hours of endless tackling of patient after patient, the ward's ceaseless hum was punctuated by the insistent ringing of Dr. Madhav's phone. A nurse, her face etched with a mix of relief and concern, approached him, a charred college ID card clutched in her hand.

"Madhav sir, we found this in the burn victim's pocket. It's mostly destroyed, but we could make out the name 'Ashwini Krishnamurty' and a phone number."

Madhav's heart quickened. Finally, a lead. He asked Nakul to handle the case. Nakul dialed the number, his fingers tracing the faint impressions on the card.

A man's voice, thick with anxiety, answered on the second ring. "Hello?"

"Mr. Krishnamurty? I'm Dr. Nakul from the Civil Hospital. We have a patient here, probably your son, with severe burns. We found your name and number on his ID card."

A choked sob echoed through the line. "Parth! Is he okay? Where is he?"

"Yes, he's in the Civil Hospital, sir, but his condition is critical. We need to discuss his medical history, any allergies, pre-existing conditions…"

Silence stretched across the line, punctuated only by the muffled sounds of the ward. "I... I don't know anything, Doctor. He's my son, Parth. He left for college this morning. We've been trying to call him since last night, but his phone was switched off!"

Nakul's brow furrowed. No medical history? No emergency contact information? How was this possible in the age of digital records and smartphones? He glanced at the overflowing stack of files on his desk, a stark reminder of the country's antiquated system. A fleeting thought of his mentor's constant complaints and stories of patient histories being available due to digitalisation in his hospital in the US had been rubbing on him too.

"Mr. Krishnamurty, I need you to come to the hospital immediately. Your son needs specialised care, and we're working on transferring him to a private facility."

As he hung up, Madhav's frustration simmered on hearing the conversation between Nakul and Ashwini. This incident highlighted the urgent need for digitalization in healthcare. If Parth's medical records had been readily available, precious time could have been saved. If emergency contact information was linked to his ID, his family could have been notified sooner. A lot of things could have been done differently. Maybe when he was just discovered in the accident spot even.

With renewed determination, Madhav navigated the labyrinthine bureaucracy, utilising every available resource to expedite Parth's transfer. He pulled strings, made calls, and leveraged his reputation to secure a bed in a private hospital's burn unit.

As Parth was wheeled out of the ward, Madhav watched, his mind racing. This close call was a stark reminder of the critical importance of development on the grassroot level. Things which are out of his hands. But as he always ensured, Madhav with unbreakable resolve, continued back to his work, his duty, catering to endless patients with a calm smile.

While Nakul was checking out, he noticed an old chap entering the ambulance along with Parth and the Paramedics. He assumed it was Ashwini and looking at the sunset, thought of three things, food, sleep and the fact that if there was any other attending other than Dr. Madhav, they wouldn't have probably even thought much of Parth's case, let alone save his life from the state he was at. Yet, he knew, Dr. Madhav would not even think about the work he did and only look forward to the hundreds of patients he has to deal with. Only then could he ensure that every patient, regardless of their socioeconomic background, received the timely and effective care they deserved. The only thing which ensured Dr. Madhav sleeps well at night.

And then he left for his hostel to sleep.

"Community, Identity, Stability" - The World State's motto, a chilling reminder of Aldous Huxley's dystopian vision, serves as a cautionary tale as we navigate the complex landscape of healthcare in India today. While the pursuit of progress and efficiency is laudable, it must not come at the cost of individual autonomy and compassion. The Indian healthcare system, much like the society it serves, is at a crossroads, grappling with the challenges of a rapidly changing world and the urgent need to adapt and evolve.

This chapter is where I can put in my expertise and speak with complete freedom as Medoc is actually placed beautifully in this chapter.

The advent of digitalization and new technologies offers a glimmer of hope, a potential pathway towards a more equitable, accessible, and efficient healthcare system. From electronic health records (EHRs) and telemedicine platforms to artificial intelligence (AI) and machine learning, these innovations have the power to transform the way healthcare is delivered and accessed in India. I'm fortunate to build myself the opportunity to work in all of these areas.

Imagine a world where every patient's medical history, from childhood immunizations to chronic disease management, is stored securely and accessible at the touch of a button. EHRs can streamline patient information, enabling seamless communication and collaboration between healthcare providers, reducing medical errors, and improving the overall quality of care.

In the vast and diverse landscape of India, where geographical barriers and socioeconomic disparities often hinder access to quality healthcare, telemedicine emerges as a beacon of hope, a bridge that spans the chasm between urban and rural communities.

This innovative approach to healthcare delivery, leveraging the power of telecommunications technology, has the potential to revolutionize the way medical services are accessed and provided, particularly in underserved areas where the shortage of healthcare professionals and infrastructure remains a persistent challenge.

Imagine a scenario where a young mother in a remote village, her child suffering from a high fever and persistent cough, can connect with a pediatrician in a major city through a simple video call. The doctor, armed with the child's medical history and a visual assessment of their condition, can provide a diagnosis, prescribe medication, and offer guidance on home care, all without the need for the mother to travel long distances or incur significant expenses. This is the transformative power of telemedicine, a technology that brings specialized medical expertise to the doorsteps of those who need it most, transcending geographical barriers and empowering individuals to take control of their health.

The potential benefits of telemedicine in India are immense. In a country where over 70% of the population resides in rural areas, where access to qualified medical professionals is often limited, telemedicine can bridge the gap between urban and rural healthcare, ensuring that even the most remote communities have access to timely and effective care. It can also reduce the burden on overcrowded urban hospitals, allowing patients with non-emergency conditions to receive consultations and follow-up care from the comfort of their homes.

Telemedicine can also play a crucial role in addressing the shortage of healthcare professionals in India. By enabling doctors and specialists to consult with patients remotely, it can optimize the utilization of existing human resources, allowing them to reach a wider patient base and provide care to those who would otherwise have limited access. This can be particularly beneficial in areas where the doctor-to-patient ratio is alarmingly low, ensuring that patients receive timely and appropriate medical attention.

Furthermore, telemedicine can be a powerful tool for preventive care and health promotion. Through remote consultations, healthcare providers can educate patients about healthy lifestyle choices, provide guidance on disease prevention, and monitor chronic conditions, empowering individuals to take proactive steps towards maintaining their health and well-being. This can lead to early detection and intervention, reducing the burden of disease and improving overall health outcomes.

The COVID-19 pandemic served as a catalyst for the rapid adoption of telemedicine in India. With lockdowns and restrictions on movement, telemedicine emerged as a lifeline for patients seeking medical advice and treatment. It enabled healthcare providers to continue providing essential services while minimizing the risk of infection, ensuring continuity of care even in the face of unprecedented challenges. The pandemic also highlighted the potential of telemedicine to address the mental health needs of the population, providing a safe and accessible platform for individuals to seek counseling and support.

However, the widespread adoption of telemedicine in India is not without its challenges. The lack of adequate digital infrastructure, particularly in rural areas, remains a significant barrier. The high cost of internet connectivity and the limited availability of smartphones and other digital devices can hinder access to telemedicine services for many. Moreover, concerns about data privacy and security, the need for standardized protocols and guidelines, and the integration of telemedicine into the existing healthcare system pose additional challenges.

Addressing these challenges will require a concerted effort from all stakeholders, including the government, the private sector, and healthcare professionals. The government must invest in expanding broadband connectivity, particularly in rural areas, and promoting digital literacy among the population. It must also create a regulatory framework that ensures the quality, safety, and ethical practice of telemedicine services.

The private sector can play a crucial role in developing and deploying innovative telemedicine solutions that cater to the specific needs of the Indian population. This could involve creating user-friendly platforms, integrating telemedicine with existing healthcare systems, and providing training and support to healthcare providers.

Healthcare professionals must also embrace the potential of telemedicine and EHRs and adapt their practices to incorporate this new modality of care delivery. This will require ongoing training and education, as well as a willingness to collaborate and innovate to ensure that telemedicine is seamlessly integrated into the continuum of care.

The journey towards a digitally empowered healthcare system in India is a long and complex one, but it is a journey that holds immense promise. By embracing the potential of telemedicine, we can bridge the gap between urban and rural healthcare, improve access to specialized care, and empower individuals to take control of their health. It is a vision of a future where healthcare is not just a privilege for the few but a fundamental right for all, where technology serves as a catalyst for positive change, and where the promise of healing and well-being reaches every corner of the nation.

At Medoc, the solution we came across was to give more power to doctors by building systems which mimicked the doctor's prescription pad and provide extremely serviceable and accountable medical voice transcription which creates prescription seemlessly along with systems for doctors to create their own templates.

This additional power motivated doctors to test the systems out and actually work together.

Moving to more pressing developments, in the realm of healthcare, where the stakes are often life and death, the advent of artificial intelligence (AI) and machine learning (ML) heralds a new era of possibilities. These transformative technologies, with their ability to analyze vast amounts of data and identify patterns invisible to the human eye, hold immense promise in revolutionizing healthcare delivery, making it more efficient, effective, and patient-centric.

AI-powered diagnostic tools, trained on massive datasets of medical images and patient records, can aid in the early detection and diagnosis of diseases, often with greater accuracy and speed than traditional methods. Imagine an AI algorithm analyzing a mammogram and identifying subtle signs of breast cancer that might be missed by a human radiologist, potentially saving lives through early intervention. Or consider an AI-powered chatbot that can triage patients based on their symptoms, providing immediate guidance and directing them to the appropriate level of care, thereby reducing the burden on overcrowded emergency rooms.

Machine learning algorithms, on the other hand, can analyze patient data to predict disease outbreaks, identify high-risk individuals, and enable personalized treatment plans. By leveraging the power of big data and predictive analytics, healthcare providers can proactively identify and address potential health issues, tailor treatments to individual needs and preferences, and ultimately improve patient outcomes.

The potential applications of Artificial Intelligence in healthcare are vast and varied. They can assist in drug discovery and development, streamlining the process and reducing costs. They can optimize hospital operations, improving efficiency and resource allocation. They can even enhance patient engagement and adherence to treatment plans through personalized reminders and virtual health coaching.

The integration of AI and ML into the Indian healthcare system has the potential to address some of its most pressing challenges. The shortage of healthcare professionals, particularly in rural areas, can be mitigated by leveraging telemedicine platforms powered by AI, enabling remote consultations and diagnosis. The burden on overworked doctors and nurses can be eased by automating routine tasks and providing decision support tools. The high cost of healthcare can be reduced through AI-driven efficiencies and personalized treatment plans that optimize resource utilization.

However, the adoption of AI and ML in healthcare is not without its challenges. Concerns about data privacy and security, the need for robust regulatory frameworks, and the potential for algorithmic bias are just a few of the hurdles that need to be addressed. Moreover, there is a need for significant investment in infrastructure, training, and capacity building to ensure that these technologies are effectively integrated into the healthcare ecosystem.

Despite these challenges, the potential benefits of AI and ML in healthcare are too significant to ignore. By embracing these transformative technologies, India can leapfrog into a new era of healthcare delivery, one that is more efficient,effective, patient-centric, and accessible to all. It is a vision of a future where technology and human expertise work in synergy to create a healthier and happier India, where the promise of healing and well-being is not a distant dream but a tangible reality for all.

The benefits of embracing digitalization in healthcare are manifold. It can improve efficiency by streamlining processes, reducing paperwork, and minimizing errors. It can reduce costs by optimizing resource allocation,preventing unnecessary tests and procedures, and improving patient adherence to treatment plans. It can enhance patient safety by providing real-time access to medical information, enabling early detection of adverse events, and facilitating better coordination of care.

Furthermore, digitalization can expand access to care, particularly in underserved areas. Telemedicine platforms can connect patients in remote locations with specialists, while mobile health applications can empower individuals to track their health parameters, manage chronic conditions, and receive personalized health advice.

However, the path to digital transformation is not without its challenges. It requires significant investment in infrastructure, training, and capacity building. There are also concerns about data privacy and security, the digital divide between urban and rural areas, and the potential for technology to exacerbate existing inequalities.

Addressing these challenges will require a concerted effort from all stakeholders, including the government, the private sector, healthcare professionals, and the community at large. It will involve developing robust policies and regulatory frameworks, investing in digital health infrastructure, and promoting digital literacy among both healthcare providers and patients.

The journey towards a digitally empowered healthcare system in India is a complex one, but it is a journey that must be undertaken with urgency and determination. By embracing the potential of technology, we can create a healthcare landscape that is not only more efficient and accessible but also more equitable and patient-centric. It is a brave new world that awaits us, one where technology serves as a catalyst for positive change, empowering individuals and communities to take control of their health and well-being.

While the potential of digitalization and new technologies to transform healthcare in India is undeniable, their adoption has been fraught with challenges, revealing a complex interplay of systemic, cultural, and economic factors. The path to a digitally empowered healthcare system is not a smooth one; it is riddled with obstacles that demand careful navigation and a multi-pronged approach.

One of the most significant barriers to digital adoption is the lack of adequate infrastructure, particularly in rural and remote areas. While urban centers boast relatively good internet connectivity and access to digital devices, vast swathes of the country remain digitally underserved. This digital divide creates a significant barrier to the implementation of technologies like telemedicine and electronic health records, limiting their reach and impact. Furthermore, even in areas with decent connectivity, the reliability and speed of internet access can be erratic, hindering the seamless flow of information and communication that is crucial for effective digital healthcare solutions.

Another challenge lies in the realm of digital literacy. While the younger generation is increasingly tech-savvy, a significant portion of the population, particularly in rural areas and among the elderly, struggles with basic digital skills. This lack of digital literacy can create barriers to accessing and utilizing digital health platforms, limiting their effectiveness and perpetuating existing inequalities in healthcare access.

A major problem which requires to be dealt with at the same time is that the very nature of healthcare information, encompassing personal details, medical histories, and treatment plans, makes it a prime target for cyberattacks and data breaches. The lack of a comprehensive data protection framework in India, coupled with the increasing sophistication of cybercriminals, has created a climate of uncertainty and apprehension, hindering the widespread adoption of digital health technologies.

The consequences of data breaches in the healthcare sector can be devastating. In 2017, the WannaCry ransomware attack crippled the UK's National Health Service (NHS), causing widespread disruption and delaying critical patient care. In 2021, a massive data breach at a leading Indian diagnostics chain exposed the personal and medical information of over 10 million patients, raising serious concerns about the security of health data in the country.

The financial implications of data breaches can be equally staggering. A 2020 study by IBM Security estimated that the average cost of a data breach in the healthcare industry is a whopping $7.13 million, the highest among all industries. This cost includes not only the immediate expenses of investigating and remediating the breach but also the long-term impact on reputation, patient trust, and potential legal liabilities.

The fear of data breaches and misuse is not limited to the healthcare sector. Other industries have also grappled with the challenges of safeguarding sensitive information in the digital age. In 2013, the retail giant Target suffered a massive data breach that exposed the credit and debit card information of over 40 million customers. In 2017, the credit reporting agency Equifax experienced a breach that compromised the personal information of over 147 million people. These incidents serve as stark reminders of the vulnerabilities of digital systems and the potential consequences of inadequate data protection measures.

The lack of a comprehensive data protection framework in India further exacerbates these concerns. While the government has taken steps to address data privacy and security through legislation such as the Personal Data Protection Bill, 2019, its implementation remains pending. This regulatory vacuum creates uncertainty and leaves both healthcare providers and patients vulnerable to data breaches and misuse.

The prevalence of cyberattacks, fueled by the increasing sophistication of cybercriminals and the lucrative nature of health data, adds another layer of complexity. Ransomware attacks, where hackers encrypt sensitive data and demand payment for its release, have become a common threat to healthcare organizations worldwide. In 2021, the US healthcare sector faced the most ransomware attacks out of any sector, according to the Federal Bureau of Investigation's Internet Crime Report.

These challenges have created a sense of hesitancy among both healthcare providers and patients when it comes to adopting digital health technologies. While the potential benefits are undeniable, the fear of data breaches and misuse can be a significant deterrent. Building trust in digital health solutions requires a multi-pronged approach that encompasses robust data protection measures, transparent data-sharing practices, and a strong regulatory framework.

The government must prioritize the implementation of a comprehensive data protection law that safeguards the privacy and security of health information. Healthcare providers must invest in cybersecurity measures, educate their staff on data protection protocols, and ensure that patient data is handled with the utmost care and confidentiality. Patients, too, must be empowered to make informed decisions about their health data, understanding the risks and benefits of sharing their information and demanding transparency from healthcare providers.

The journey towards a digitally empowered healthcare system in India is a complex one, fraught with challenges and uncertainties. But it is a journey that must be undertaken with courage and determination. By addressing the concerns around data privacy and security, we can unlock the full potential of digital health technologies, creating a healthcare landscape that is not only more efficient and accessible but also more secure and trustworthy.

Perhaps the most formidable barrier to digital adoption lies in the realm of human behavior and organizational culture. Many healthcare professionals, accustomed to traditional methods of practice, are resistant to change and apprehensive about embracing new technologies. The perceived complexity of digital systems, the learning curve associated with their adoption, and the fear of obsolescence can all contribute to this resistance. Moreover, some healthcare providers,particularly in the private sector, may be reluctant to invest in digital infrastructure due to the high upfront costs and the perceived lack of immediate financial returns.

The ground reality in many healthcare settings reveals a stark contrast between the promise of technology and its actual implementation. Paper-based records continue to dominate, leading to inefficiencies, errors, and delays in patient care. Communication between healthcare providers is often fragmented and reliant on outdated methods, hindering collaboration and coordination of care. The potential of technology to improve efficiency, reduce costs, and enhance patient outcomes remains largely untapped.

While the potential benefits of digital transformation in healthcare are undeniable, the path to adoption is often fraught with resistance, particularly among healthcare professionals who have long relied on traditional methods of practice.This reluctance to embrace change is often rooted in a deep-seated belief in the superiority of familiar practices.

Moreover, the hierarchical structure of the medical profession in India, where senior doctors often wield significant influence, can further impede the adoption of new technologies. Younger doctors and healthcare professionals, who may be more receptive to innovation, might hesitate to challenge the established norms and practices, fearing repercussions or a loss of professional standing.

The value balance in many healthcare settings is thus tilted towards familiar practices, even when evidence suggests that newer, technologically advanced approaches may be more effective or efficient. This reluctance to embrace change can stifle innovation and hinder progress towards a more patient-centric and technologically advanced healthcare system.

The challenges of digital adoption are not limited to healthcare professionals alone. Patients, too, may exhibit a degree of skepticism or apprehension towards new technologies. This can stem from a lack of awareness about the benefits of digital health solutions, concerns about data privacy and security, or simply a preference for traditional methods of care.Building trust and confidence in digital health technologies will require a concerted effort to educate and empower both healthcare providers and patients.

The journey towards digital transformation in Indian healthcare is thus a delicate balancing act, one that requires navigating the complexities of tradition, culture, and human behavior. It demands a nuanced approach that respects the wisdom of the past while embracing the possibilities of the future. It calls for a collaborative effort between policymakers, healthcare professionals, technology providers, and the community at large to create a healthcare system that is both technologically advanced and culturally sensitive, one that harnesses the power of innovation to deliver quality care to all, while preserving the essence of the human touch that lies at the heart of healing.

The journey towards a digitally empowered healthcare system in India is a complex and multifaceted odyssey, fraught with challenges and uncertainties. It is not merely a matter of investing in infrastructure and technology; it requires a profound shift in mindset and organizational culture, a willingness to embrace change, to challenge the status quo, and to prioritize patient welfare over entrenched practices.

The road ahead is long and winding, but the destination is clear: a future where technology serves as a catalyst for positive change, empowering individuals and communities to take control of their health and well-being. It is a vision of a healthcare system that is not only more efficient and accessible but also more equitable and patient-centric.

India's healthcare system, while battling a multitude of challenges, can glean valuable insights from successful healthcare models around the world that have effectively tackled similar issues. By studying and contrasting these models with India's current system, we can identify potential solutions and best practices that can be adapted and implemented to pave the way for a more accessible, equitable, and efficient healthcare system in India.

The NHS, founded in 1948, is a shining example of a universal healthcare system that provides comprehensive medical care to all UK residents, regardless of their ability to pay. It is funded primarily through general taxation, ensuring that healthcare is a right, not a privilege. The NHS offers a wide range of services, including primary care, hospital care, mental health services, and dental care, free at the point of use. It is renowned for its focus on preventive care, early diagnosis, and community-based services.

While India has a network of public healthcare facilities, they are often overburdened, understaffed, and lack essential resources. The lack of universal healthcare coverage and the high out-of-pocket expenditure in India create significant barriers to access, particularly for the poor and vulnerable. The NHS model, with its emphasis on universal coverage and free healthcare at the point of use, offers a potential pathway for India to achieve equitable healthcare access for all its citizens.

Canada's healthcare system is a publicly funded, single-payer system that provides universal coverage to all Canadian citizens and permanent residents. While the federal government sets national standards, the provinces and territories are responsible for administering and delivering healthcare services. The Canadian system covers medically necessary hospital and physician services, ensuring that Canadians have access to essential care without financial hardship. It also emphasizes preventive care and health promotion.

While India has a mix of public and private healthcare providers, the public sector is often underfunded and overburdened, while the private sector is largely unregulated and unaffordable for many. The Canadian model, with its emphasis on universal coverage and a strong public healthcare system, offers insights into how India can strengthen its public healthcare infrastructure and ensure equitable access to care.

Germany's healthcare system is a multi-payer model based on social health insurance. It is mandatory for all residents to have health insurance, either through statutory health insurance funds or private health insurance. The system is funded through a combination of employer and employee contributions, as well as government subsidies. The German system provides comprehensive coverage for a wide range of medical services, including preventive care, hospital care, mental health services, and prescription drugs. It also emphasizes patient choice and allows for private healthcare providers to operate alongside the statutory health insurance funds.

While India has a growing private health insurance market, it is largely unregulated and unaffordable for many. The lack of mandatory health insurance and the high out-of-pocket expenditure leave a significant portion of the population uninsured and vulnerable to financial hardship. The German model, with its emphasis on mandatory health insurance and a mix of public and private providers, offers insights into how India can expand health insurance coverage and create a more regulated and competitive healthcare market.

While the healthcare models of the UK, Canada, and Germany differ in their structure and funding mechanisms, they share some common principles that can be valuable for India's healthcare reform efforts.

- **Universal Coverage**: Ensuring that all citizens have access to essential healthcare services, regardless of their ability to pay, is a fundamental principle of successful healthcare systems. India can achieve this through a combination of government-sponsored schemes, community-based health insurance models, and innovative micro-insurance products.

- **Strong Public Healthcare Infrastructure**: A robust public healthcare system is essential for providing equitable access to care, particularly for the poor and vulnerable. India needs to invest significantly in building and upgrading public healthcare facilities, training and retaining healthcare professionals, and improving the quality of care in the public sector.

- **Regulation and Quality Assurance**: A well-regulated healthcare market, with clear standards for quality and safety, is crucial for protecting patients and ensuring that they receive the best possible care. India needs to strengthen its regulatory framework for both public and private healthcare providers, implement robust quality assurance mechanisms, and promote transparency and accountability.

- **Emphasis on Preventive Care and Health Promotion**: Investing in preventive care and health promotion can help reduce the burden of disease and improve health outcomes. India needs to prioritize public health initiatives, such as immunization programs, health education campaigns, and screenings for early detection of diseases.

- **Technology and Innovation**: Leveraging technology and innovation can help improve the efficiency and effectiveness of healthcare delivery. India can harness the power of telemedicine, mobile health clinics, and electronic health records to expand access to care, improve patient outcomes, and reduce costs.

In this brave new world, the boundaries between urban and rural healthcare will blur, as telemedicine bridges the gap and brings specialized care to the remotest corners of the nation. The power of artificial intelligence and machine learning will be harnessed to predict disease outbreaks, personalize treatment plans, and revolutionize diagnostics.Electronic health records will streamline patient information, enabling seamless communication and collaboration between healthcare providers, reducing medical errors, and improving the overall quality of care.

But this transformation will not happen overnight. It will require a concerted effort from all stakeholders, from policymakers and healthcare professionals to technology providers and patients themselves. It will demand a willingness to learn, to adapt, and to embrace the possibilities that technology offers. It will also necessitate a commitment to addressing the challenges of data privacy and security, the digital divide, and the potential for technology to exacerbate existing inequalities.

As we stand on the cusp of this new era, let us embrace the challenges and opportunities that lie ahead. Let us work together, with unwavering dedication and a shared vision, to create a healthcare system that is truly responsive to the needs of the 21st century. Let us leverage the power of technology to deliver quality care to all, regardless of their location or socioeconomic status. Let us build a healthcare system that is not just technologically advanced, but also compassionate, equitable, and accessible to all.

The world needs to move towards preventive medicine and more importantly towards personalized medicine and the only way we can ensure best results is through extensive research and development in the country itself.

Let us aim for a healthier India, where technology empowers us to achieve the seemingly impossible. Let us translate those dreams into thoughts, and those thoughts into action, creating a future where healthcare is not just a privilege but a fundamental right for all.

The pursuit of a just and equitable healthcare system, while a noble and necessary endeavor, is but one facet of the larger tapestry of human development. As we emerge from the depths of the Inferno, where the challenges and complexities of healthcare in India have been laid bare, we turn our gaze towards another crucial pillar of society:education.

In the chapters that follow, we will delve into the complexities of the Indian education system, exploring its triumphs and tribulations, its hopes and its despair. We will witness the struggles of students navigating a system that often prioritizes conformity over creativity, rote learning over critical thinking, and academic success over holistic development. We will also celebrate the stories of those who have dared to challenge the status quo, to break free from the shackles of convention, and to forge their own paths towards a more fulfilling and meaningful education.

Through the lens of Parth's journey, we will explore the transformative power of education, its ability to ignite passions,spark innovation, and empower individuals to become agents of change. We will examine the role of technology in shaping the future of education, the importance of mentorship and guidance, and the need for a more inclusive and equitable learning environment.

As we embark on this new chapter, let us carry with us the lessons learned from the Inferno, the recognition that true progress lies in addressing the root causes of inequality and empowering individuals to take control of their own destinies. Let us dive deeper into the contrast, strive to create an education system that not only imparts knowledge but also nurtures creativity,critical thinking, and a lifelong love for learning. Let us build a future where education is not just a privilege but a fundamental right for all, a catalyst for personal growth, societal transformation, and a brighter, more equitable India.

Fahrenheit 451

"Cram them full of non-combustible data, chock them so damned full of 'facts' they feel stuffed, but absolutely 'brilliant' with information. Then they'll feel they're thinking, they'll get a sense of motion without moving. And they'll be happy, because facts of that sort don't change."

- Ray Bradbury in Fahrenheit 451

Great Expectations

Parth's eyelids fluttered open, and a blinding light assaulted his senses. He squinted, his vision slowly adjusting to reveal the worried faces of his parents hovering above him. Relief washed over him, a fleeting moment of warmth amidst the searing pain that engulfed his body. But as he closed his eyes, the light gave way to a relentless torrent of memories, each one a shard of regret piercing his heart.

He saw himself as a child, a bundle of boundless energy, his laughter echoing through the playground as he chased a volleyball, his dreams soaring high above the net. The world was a playground, and he was its fearless explorer. Those were the halcyon days, filled with the innocence of youth and the promise of endless possibilities.

Then came the stark transition, the playground replaced by the classroom. The once-vibrant boy was now a solitary figure, hunched over textbooks, his spirit gradually dimming beneath the weight of academic expectations. The carefree laughter was replaced by the ticking clock of exams and the looming shadow of parental expectations. His passion for the sport, once a source of joy and fulfilment, was sacrificed at the altar of academic success, a painful compromise that echoed through the corridors of his memory.

The flashbacks continued, painting a bleak picture of his life. He saw himself hunched over a desk, the harsh glow of a lamp casting long shadows across his weary face. He relived the countless hours spent preparing for entrance exams, the endless cycle of studying, failing, and starting all over again. The disappointment in his parents' eyes, the pitying glances of his friends, the crushing weight of his own perceived inadequacy - it all came flooding back, a tidal wave of self-reproach.

Then came the private engineering college, a gilded cage purchased with his parents' hard-earned money. He saw himself sitting in dimly lit classrooms, struggling to keep up with the lectures, his mind a jumbled mess of formulas and theories. The pressure to succeed, to secure a high-paying job, hung over him like a dark cloud, suffocating his every ambition.

And then, darkness.

When Parth opened his eyes again, the harsh light of the hospital room pierced through his clouded vision. He saw his mother and father standing by the door, their faces etched with worry, their tears a silent testament to their love. His body, swathed in bandages, felt heavy and alien, an IV drip snaking its way into his arm. The pain was a constant companion, a dull ache punctuated by sharp stabs of agony.

He closed his eyes once more, seeking refuge in the merciful embrace of sleep. But even in the darkness, the memories continued to haunt him. He saw missed opportunities, wasted potential, and a future that seemed to slip further away with each passing day.

Then, a glimmer of hope. He remembered the joy of the volleyball court, the thrill of the chase, the camaraderie of his teammates. He remembered the pride in his parents' eyes when he excelled in his studies, the feeling of accomplishment that came with overcoming a challenge.

He opened his eyes again, his gaze falling on his parents as they spoke to the doctor through the glass door. Their voices were muffled, but their love for him was unmistakable. A flicker of determination ignited in his heart. He would fight. He would overcome this setback, just as he had overcome countless others. And when he emerged from this ordeal, he would find his own path, one that led to a future filled with purpose and fulfilment.

With a newfound sense of resolve, Parth closed his eyes once more, allowing the gentle lull of sleep to carry him away. Amidst all this, deep inside, he has a last fleeting thought: What if he fails his parent's expectation to recover from this, again?

Whenever we talk about building resources, be it for healthcare, or any sector of the world, the one thing which is crucial to understand is healthcare.

As a recent student and speaking from the point of view of the youth of this nation, I'll say a statement very clearly and then in this entire section, build it in perspective.

The Indian Education System has failed. It's not a let's repaint it with a policy kind of situation, and it's not the problem of the administration or the government alone. We as a society, as a nation, have successfully broken our own education system in our hopes and aspirations and are not ready to take the blame for it. This isn't something that needs a bill to be passed or even policies to be changed honestly. Just read this and the following chapters clearly and with an open mind, and try your best to resist without biases.

As the narrative of countless Indian students' lives unfolds, the harsh realities of the Indian education system often shatter these great expectations, leaving many feeling disillusioned, frustrated, and trapped in a cycle of conformity and unfulfilled potential.

The Indian education system, much like the character of Miss Havisham in Dickens' novel, clings to outdated practices and rigid structures, its grandeur tarnished by a relentless focus on rote learning and standardized testing. It is a system that often prioritizes conformity over creativity, obedience over critical thinking, and academic success over holistic development. In this unforgiving landscape, students are often reduced to mere vessels for information, their unique talents and passions stifled beneath the weight of societal expectations.

The pressure to excel academically, to secure admission to prestigious institutions, and to land lucrative jobs, casts a long shadow over the lives of young people in India. The pursuit of grades and accolades becomes an all-consuming obsession, leaving little room for exploration, experimentation, and the cultivation of a genuine love for learning. The classroom, once a vibrant space for intellectual curiosity and creative expression, transforms into a battleground where students compete for limited resources and recognition.

The dichotomy of Indian parenting in today's date is a tragic comedy itself where on one end there is an outer layer of presenting with no expectations and a deeper heart filled with countless expectations. What that does is take away accountability from the parents towards the pressure the child is facing, not only on yourself, but also from the ward, and then at the same time creating an environment of pressure.

And honestly speaking, this relentless focus on academic achievement often comes at a heavy cost. The mental and emotional well-being of students is frequently neglected, as they grapple with anxiety, stress, and the fear of failure. The pressure doesn't come from the Central Board of Secondary Education or the National Testing Agency. The pressure to conform to societal norms and expectations can stifle individuality and creativity, leaving many feeling lost and disconnected from their true selves and questioning their lives.

Moreover, the education system's disconnect from the realities of the 21st-century workplace further exacerbates the challenges faced by students. The skills and knowledge imparted in classrooms often fail to align with the demands of the modern job market, leaving graduates ill-equipped to navigate the complexities of the professional world. This is often called the industry-academia gap and used by various universities and colleges to advertise their events while being at the center of the entire circus of creating this gap in the first place. If the industry-academia gap could be resolved in one semester of training and three to four seminars, we would have a workforce, and not children trying to navigate the industry. The emphasis on theoretical knowledge over practical skills, and the lack of opportunities for experiential learning, create a mismatch that hinders the transition from academia to the workforce.

The consequences of this flawed system are far-reaching. It perpetuates a cycle of inequality, where those from privileged backgrounds, with access to better resources and opportunities, are more likely to succeed, while those from marginalized communities are left behind. It stifles innovation and creativity, hindering the development of a truly knowledge-based society. And most importantly, it robs countless young people of the joy of learning, replacing it with a sense of dread and disillusionment.

As we navigate the complexities of the Indian education system, let us remember the words of Rabindranath Tagore, who said, "The highest education is that which does not merely give us information but makes our life in harmony with existence." Unfortunately, what we have no is untrained teachers working towards building a bunch of students who have their notebooks completed and marked with their red pens on the respective dates they're assigned along with regimented examinations checked on the basis of a checklist.

Students actually consider their teachers, or at least one of the many teachers they encounter, as a role model. But unfortunately, India has a severe shortage of teachers, despite having an oversupply of professors and lecturers.

The Indian education system, despite its rich history and contributions to the world, is often criticized for its rigid structure, intense focus on rote learning and exams, and a lack of emphasis on creativity and critical thinking. This pressure-cooker environment places immense academic stress on students, affecting their mental and physical health and hindering their holistic development. This article delves into the various academic pressures faced by Indian students, exploring their root causes and potential solutions to create a more nurturing and empowering learning environment.

The Indian education system has long been characterized by its obsession with exams. From a young age, students are conditioned to view exams as the ultimate measure of their intelligence and worth. This creates a culture of intense competition, where students are constantly under pressure to outperform their peers and secure top ranks.

It is so unfortunate to see how students with extreme calibre and talent are scared of exams and measure their worthiness with the numbers they're given on the basis of what they learn from a set syllabus when in reality, they could do so much more.

The pressure to excel in exams is relentless, starting from primary school and intensifying as students progress to higher grades. The constant emphasis on grades and ranks often overshadows the joy of learning and the pursuit of knowledge for its own sake. Students are driven by the fear of failure and the desire to meet the expectations of their parents, teachers, and society.

The exam-centric culture encourages rote learning, where students memorize facts and figures without necessarily understanding the underlying concepts. This approach stifles creativity, critical thinking, and problem-solving skills, essential attributes for success in the 21st century. The pressure to excel in exams has spawned a thriving coaching industry, where students spend countless hours after school attending extra classes and tutorials. This further adds to their workload and leaves them with little time for rest, recreation, or pursuing their interests.

The Indian curriculum, particularly in the sciences and mathematics, is often criticized for its rigidity and lack of flexibility. The focus on memorization and regurgitation of information leaves little room for exploration, experimentation, and creative expression. Students have limited choice in their subjects, especially in the crucial higher secondary years when they are expected to specialize in science or commerce streams. This can stifle their interests and passions, forcing them to pursue paths they may not be genuinely inclined towards.

The curriculum often adopts a one-size-fits-all approach, neglecting the diverse learning styles and abilities of students. This can lead to frustration and disengagement, particularly for students who learn best through hands-on activities, projects, or creative pursuits. The curriculum in some subjects is often outdated and fails to keep pace with the rapidly changing world.

This can leave students ill-equipped to face the challenges of the 21st century, where adaptability, innovation, and problem-solving skills are paramount. Information is today available so quickly.

I was sitting recently with my sister, trying to solve a problem when just after I was done reading the problem in 2-3 minutes, my 13 year old cousin gave the answer to a class 12th problem. How? He just typed in on ChatGPT. It was such an eye-opener to see how the upcoming generation is going to fail in exams for sure, but are going to excel in life, if they can overcome their depression and anxiety, that is.

The Indian education system's emphasis on rote learning and exams often comes at the expense of nurturing creativity and critical thinking skills. These essential skills are crucial for innovation, problem-solving, and adapting to a rapidly changing world. Creative pursuits, such as art, music, and drama, are often viewed as extracurricular activities and given less importance than academic subjects. This sends a message to students that creativity is not valued or essential for success.

The focus on memorization and regurgitation of information discourages students from questioning, analyzing, and evaluating information critically. This can hinder their ability to think independently, form their own opinions, and make informed decisions. The pressure to conform to societal expectations and follow the beaten path often stifles individuality and creativity. Students are discouraged from taking risks, challenging the status quo, and pursuing unconventional paths.

The relentless academic pressure on Indian students takes a toll on their mental and physical health. Anxiety, depression, sleep deprivation, and even suicide are alarmingly prevalent among students. The constant pressure to perform, the fear of failure, and the lack of support can lead to anxiety, depression, and other mental health issues. Studies have shown that Indian students have one of the highest rates of depression and suicide in the world.

The long hours of studying, lack of sleep, and unhealthy eating habits can also lead to physical health problems such as obesity, back pain, and eye strain. The relentless pursuit of academic success often robs students of their childhood. They have little time for play, recreation, or pursuing their interests, leading to a sense of isolation, burnout, and a loss of joy in learning.

I work 16 to 18 hours a day on Medoc which has resulted in severe anxiety and depression at times. It has also resulted in extreme fatigue and burnout to the level that it became well known to my peers that I'm going to fall sick at least twice in a month, and then hit my productivity on a hard pause. But the routine involves various activities. As a student preparing for a competitive exam, there is no other activity. It's purely sedentary.

Stress, a natural response to challenging situations, is a ubiquitous experience for Indian students. The pressure to excel in exams, meet societal expectations, and navigate a demanding curriculum creates a chronic state of stress that can have far-reaching consequences.

The fear of failure, the constant comparison with peers, and the high stakes associated with exams can trigger performance anxiety, a debilitating condition that hampers learning and can lead to panic attacks and other physical symptoms. The expectations of parents, teachers, and society often weigh heavily on students, creating a sense of obligation to succeed at any cost. This can lead to feelings of inadequacy, self-doubt, and a fear of disappointing others. Balancing academics with extracurricular activities, coaching classes, and family commitments can be overwhelming for students, leaving them with little time for rest and relaxation. This constant juggling act can lead to chronic stress and exhaustion.

Anxiety, a feeling of worry, nervousness, or unease, is another common mental health challenge faced by Indian students. The uncertainties associated with exams, future career prospects, and the pressure to conform to societal norms can trigger anxiety disorders that significantly impact their lives. The fear of exams can spiral into a full-blown anxiety disorder, characterized by excessive worry, restlessness, difficulty concentrating, and physical symptoms such as palpitations and shortness of breath.

This can severely impact a student's ability to perform well in exams, creating a vicious cycle of anxiety and underachievement. The competitive environment in schools and colleges can lead to social anxiety and peer pressure, where students constantly compare themselves to others and feel the need to fit in. This can lead to feelings of isolation, low self-esteem, and a fear of social judgment. The uncertainty surrounding future career prospects, coupled with the pressure to choose the "right" path, can trigger anxiety about the future. This can lead to indecisiveness, procrastination, and a sense of hopelessness.

Depression, a mood disorder characterized by persistent feelings of sadness, hopelessness, and a loss of interest in activities, is a serious mental health concern affecting many Indian students. The relentless academic pressures, coupled with a lack of support and understanding, can push students into a state of depression. The constant pressure to perform, the fear of failure, and the lack of control over their academic lives can lead to feelings of helplessness and hopelessness.

Students may feel trapped in a cycle of stress and anxiety, unable to see a way out. The constant comparison with peers and the emphasis on academic achievements can erode a student's sense of self-worth. They may start to believe that their value is solely determined by their grades and ranks, leading to feelings of inadequacy and low self-esteem. Depression often leads to social withdrawal and isolation, as students may feel ashamed or embarrassed about their struggles. This can further exacerbate their feelings of loneliness and hopelessness.

Addressing the mental health crisis among Indian students requires a multi-pronged approach that involves creating a more supportive and nurturing learning environment, promoting mental health awareness, and providing accessible and affordable mental healthcare services. The education system needs to be reformed to prioritize holistic development, reduce academic pressure, and promote mental well-being.

This includes revamping the curriculum, shifting the focus from exams, and promoting creativity and critical thinking. Schools need to create a safe and supportive environment where students feel comfortable seeking help and talking about their mental health struggles.

Mental health professionals should be available in schools to provide counseling and support to students. Awareness campaigns and educational programs need to be implemented to destigmatize mental health issues and encourage students to seek help. Parents and teachers also need to be educated about the signs and symptoms of mental health challenges so they can provide timely support to students.

Accessible and affordable mental healthcare services need to be made available to all students, regardless of their socioeconomic background. This includes increasing the number of mental health professionals, establishing helplines and online counseling services, and integrating mental health education into the curriculum.

Transforming India's education system to prioritize holistic development and reduce academic pressure requires a multi-pronged approach involving policymakers, educators, parents, and students themselves. The curriculum needs to be revamped to focus on conceptual understanding, critical thinking, and problem-solving skills. It should also provide more flexibility and choice for students, allowing them to pursue their interests and passions. The emphasis on exams needs to be reduced, and alternative assessment methods, such as projects, presentations, and portfolios, should be adopted.

This will encourage students to focus on learning rather than just memorizing for exams. Creative pursuits, such as art, music, and drama, should be integrated into the curriculum and given equal importance as academic subjects. Critical thinking skills should be nurtured through discussions, debates, and open-ended questions.

Schools and teachers need to create a supportive and nurturing learning environment where students feel safe to express themselves, ask questions, and make mistakes. Mental health support services should be readily available to address the emotional and psychological needs of students. Parents need to be educated about the harmful effects of excessive academic pressure and encouraged to support their children's holistic development. They should also be encouraged to set realistic expectations and prioritize their children's well-being over academic achievements.

The core issue of all these issues have resulted in a compounded problem in today's time:

A deeply ingrained cultural preference for "safe" and prestigious career paths, such as engineering, medicine, and law, often overshadows individual passions and aptitudes. This article delves into the complexities of these societal expectations, exploring their origins, their impact on students, and the urgent need for a more holistic approach to education and career guidance.

The societal expectations surrounding education and career choices in India cast a long shadow over the aspirations of countless students. Deeply rooted in cultural norms and historical traditions, these expectations often steer young minds towards perceived "safe" and prestigious paths, such as engineering, medicine, and law. While these professions undoubtedly offer stability and social recognition, the relentless pressure to conform can stifle individuality, creativity,and the pursuit of true passions.

The preference for these established career paths stems from a complex interplay of factors. Historically, India, with its vast population and limited resources, has valued professions that guarantee a stable income and social standing. This emphasis on security is further reinforced by the legacy of the joint family system, where the collective well-being of the family often trumps individual desires. Children are frequently encouraged to prioritize careers that contribute to the family's financial security and uphold its social image, even if it means compromising their personal interests.

Furthermore, the pervasive fear of failure in Indian society acts as a deterrent for students contemplating unconventional paths. The uncertainty associated with careers in the arts, humanities, or entrepreneurship is often perceived as a risk too great to take. This fear, combined with societal pressure, often compels students to opt for the well-trodden paths, regardless of their innate talents or inclinations.

The repercussions of this conformity are far-reaching and profound. The constant pressure to fit into predefined molds can suffocate individuality and creativity. Students may find themselves suppressing their true passions and talents to appease the expectations of their families and society. This internal conflict can lead to a sense of frustration,disengagement, and a diminished sense of self-worth.

The pursuit of "safe" careers often translates into an intense academic pressure cooker, where students are compelled to focus on subjects that may not align with their interests or aptitudes. This can lead to stress, burnout, and a diminished joy of learning, ultimately hindering their holistic development.

Moreover, the fear of making the "wrong" career choice can create a paralyzing anxiety for students. The multitude of options, coupled with the pressure to succeed, can leave them feeling overwhelmed and trapped. The fear of disappointing their loved ones can further exacerbate this anxiety, manifesting in both physical and emotional distress.In extreme cases, the weight of these expectations can even lead to depression and a sense of hopelessness.

The societal pressure to conform also results in missed opportunities. Talented artists, musicians, writers, and entrepreneurs may never discover their true calling, their potential lying dormant beneath the weight of societal expectations.

The stories of individuals who sacrificed their passions for societal approval are a poignant reminder of the human cost of conformity. The engineer who yearned to paint, the doctor who longed to teach – these are just a few examples of the countless dreams that remain unfulfilled due to the pressure to conform.

To address these challenges, India needs to reimagine its approach to education and career guidance. It is imperative to create a system that recognizes and nurtures individual talents and passions, rather than forcing students into predefined molds. Early career guidance programs, starting from school, can play a crucial role in helping students explore various career options and make informed choices based on their interests and aptitudes. This can help break the stereotype of "safe" careers and encourage students to embrace their unique talents and passions.

Schools and colleges should foster an environment that encourages creative pursuits. Providing ample opportunities for students to engage in art, music, drama, and sports can help them discover their hidden talents and foster a sense of accomplishment beyond academics.

Moreover, the curriculum needs to be revamped to emphasize critical thinking and problem-solving skills, rather than just rote learning and memorization. Equipping students with these essential skills will empower them to navigate the complexities of the 21st century, regardless of their chosen career path.

Perhaps most importantly, parents, teachers, and society at large need to cultivate a supportive and encouraging environment for students to explore their potential and pursue their dreams. It is essential to challenge stereotypes,celebrate diverse talents, and provide mentorship and guidance to students as they embark on their journey of self-discovery.

In conclusion, the societal expectations placed on Indian students, while rooted in good intentions, can often have a detrimental impact on their mental health, academic choices, and overall well-being. It is time to break free from the shackles of conformity and embrace a more holistic approach to education and career guidance. By nurturing individual talents, promoting creativity, and fostering a supportive environment, we can empower students to choose their own path and realize their full potential.

This shift will not only lead to happier and more fulfilled individuals but also contribute to a more diverse and dynamic workforce that is better equipped to meet the challenges of the 21st century. It is time to empower students to follow their dreams, regardless of societal expectations, and create a future where individuality and passion are celebrated, not suppressed.

You might say that all of the above is already available in the grandiose school which looks like a five star hotel and charges more money.

The Education sector has had the biggest inflation of all times. And I'm talking about atleast 300% 5 year CAGR if you want it in clear terms.

The Indian education system, while a source of national pride, stands at a crossroads. The relentless pressure to conform,the exam-centric culture, and the neglect of creativity and critical thinking skills have created a system that, while producing academically proficient individuals, often stifles individuality, fosters anxiety, and perpetuates a cycle of conformity. It is imperative to recognize that true progress lies not in churning out a generation of rote learners but in nurturing a generation of thinkers, innovators, and problem-solvers who can lead India into the 21st century with confidence and purpose.

The challenges are immense, but the stakes are even higher. The future of India rests on the shoulders of its youth, and it is our responsibility to provide them with an education system that empowers them to reach their full potential.

The journey towards a more holistic and empowering education system will undoubtedly be arduous, but it is a journey that we must embark on with urgency and determination. The next chapter awaits, where we will delve deeper into the complexities of these issues and explore potential solutions to create an education system that truly serves the needs of our students and paves the way for a brighter future for India.

Lord of the Flies

Parth's eyelids fluttered open, the world a hazy blur of muted colors and hushed voices. His gaze settled on his elder sister, Mohini, her silhouette a familiar comfort amidst the sterile confines of the hospital room. She stood beside their mother, their conversation a low murmur that danced on the edge of Parth's consciousness. He remained still, his eyes closed, feigning sleep, yet every word spoken by his beloved sister resonated deep within him.

"I'm so tired of this job, Ma," Mohini's voice, laced with frustration, broke the silence. "It's not what I ever wanted. It's not who I am. I don't even understand what I'm doing anymore. It's not hard, it's just not interesting. And that feels worse"

Their mother's response was gentle, yet tinged with a hint of resignation. "But beta, you were the one who chose this path. You excelled in your studies, got into a good college..."

"Exactly!" Mohini's voice rose, her words sharp with pent-up emotion. "I was good at what the system told me to be good at. I jumped through all the hoops, got the grades, and landed a 'respectable' job. But it's not fulfilling. It's not me."

She paused, her voice softening as she continued. "How was I supposed to know what I truly wanted when I was in tenth grade, or even twelfth? The education system doesn't prepare you for the real world. It's all about rote learning and exams, not about discovering your passions or exploring your potential. Moreover, what I was taught and what I'm doing is completely different."

Their mother sighed, her gaze shifting towards Parth, who lay silently on the bed, his bandaged form a stark reminder of the harsh realities of life. Mohini followed her mother's gaze, her expression softening. "Is he awake? I don't like him like this." she whispered.

Their mother shook her head. "No, he's still resting. The doctor said he'll be fine. Fractures will take a couple of months of Physiotherapy. They also want him to visit a therapist. Other than that, his burn wounds will be fine. Shouldn't scar much, hopefully. Thank God for sending a couple passing by going to the hospital because her wife was in labor. They discovered him and took him there too."

Mohini's voice dropped to a barely audible murmur. "Any news from the police, Ma?"

A shadow crossed their mother's face. "Not much, beta. The warden confirmed that Parth never reached the hostel.They found a beggar near the scene, but he hasn't been much help. Your father has gone to the station to get an update."

Parth's heart ached as he listened to their conversation, every word a painful echo of his own struggles. He too had been a victim of the system, forced to conform to its rigid expectations, his dreams and aspirations crushed beneath the weight of societal pressures. The education system had failed him, just as it had failed his sister along with endless others. It had left them ill-equipped to navigate the complexities of the real world, their potential untapped, their passions unfulfilled.

As he drifted back into the hazy realm of sleep, Parth couldn't help but wonder if there was a different path, a world where education nurtured dreams instead of stifling them, where young minds were encouraged to explore, create, and discover their true calling. But for now, those dreams remained distant, overshadowed by the harsh realities of his present circumstances.

I'll get to primary education as we proceed in this chapter, but, let's start with breaking down the gold medals of our society first. Degrees, Diplomas and Professional Training. College and university based education is something which has been extremely valued for the longest time. A degree is given its value based on the amount of things you learn and pride in structure and flexibility along with specialization in a specific industry.

The traditional college degree, long considered a ticket to success and a cornerstone of one's professional journey, is increasingly losing its relevance. As the world of work evolves at a rapid pace, fueled by technological advancements and shifting industry demands, the gap between what is taught in our colleges and what is required in the real world is growing wider by the day. So, what is changing now and why am I saying that the value of a degree is falling?

Honestly, the only value a degree has in today's time is of societal value and bragging rights. It's reduced down to just conversation. The entire gist of learning and experience has in the last 15-20 years been completely dusted aside very jokingly and sparsely.

When I asked various people in my network, I got to know that people think there are various possible issues.

Some said that the curriculums are outdated. While the world has seen massive technological advancements, the education system has largely failed to keep up. Courses that were once cutting-edge are now obsolete, and students are often left studying material that has little relevance to the modern job market.

Others say that the problem is in Private colleges mass producing uninterested graduates who are under heavy pressure to earn a return of investment in the field and industry they are not even interested in.

While there are some people who say that the issue lies in the fact that there's a disconnect between industry and academia, where neither is ready to bend to the requirements of the other as it's apparently too much work in the scattered and rigid systems. The rapid pace of change in the business world, driven by digital transformation, globalization, and the rise of new industries, has left many academic institutions struggling to keep up. The result is a generation of graduates who are ill-prepared for the demands of the modern workplace.

Some people from my network in universities even went far enough to say that the problem lies with higher education governing authorities like UGC and AICTE. They say that the industry demands degrees which are "accredited."

Another thought process was that there's a major issue in India, China, Sri Lanka, Pakistan etc. around population per capita and demand-supply of work in every industry.

In my opinion, the sole reason why these precious degrees are losing their value is actually because of the Internet. Ever since information has become so openly available and accessible, it has become easy for anyone to master the skills they wish to work in. The job market has become open and most importantly, with the upcoming rise of the "Gig Economy", we see a continuous increase in democratization of resources and increasing value of skills over a "piece of paper" degree.

Let's explore a world without college degrees and conventional forms of employment:

The first major thing which will happen is all the uncles and aunties of the world will not have anything to brag about their nieces and nephews achievements of bagging a degree or pointing out how their neighbour's son is unemployed even after their degree from such a prestigious institution paying enough money to construct a home. Universities and Colleges which are right now built with such huge infrastructure will end up looking for other forms of income. But wait, I have something for them as well in this article itself, and it's better than scamming a million students over a decade.

Parents will end up saving lakhs. I wish the Indian middle class was good enough at saving money as much as they do to pay their children's fees. The high fees is nothing but the result of the demand created by the parents to providing endless opportunities to their wards out of pure love, care and compassion.

All these pure feelings of a parent are beautifully exploited first by EdTech companies like Byju's (May it's soul rest in peace and case studies). Then they are exploited for the same love and worry by coaching centres like Allen, FIITJEE, Akash and all these huge players. Some even go far enough to play at scale with their vast distribution like PhysicsWallah and Unacademy.

After all this as well, when they see that their child couldn't clear an exam, whatever it might be, JEE, NEET or whatever, they look for the next best thing for them. Enters private universities. Mark my word, if you think the coaching industry sucks your hard earned money, blood, sweat and patience, these universities will not even let your skin and hair aside.

Why do parents pay so much and do so much? Because they've struggled their entire life. They've come up in their lives from humble beginnings to whatever they have today. They only want for their children to lead a comfortable, secure life on their own feet and end up giving a lot of padding for the same. These universities promise the cushions for the padding. All in all, in a world without colleges, there will be peace. And… they just don't want you to know that.

So, where do these universities go now? In this new world, the colleges I'm so unfairly beating up with my words still have a role. It's just not policing around students over 75% attendances and pending fees and uniform codes.

Whatever anyone (including myself) says, colleges have invested money. If they fire around 80% of their useless professors and admin staff, they will have enough money to regularly maintain their labs and create an amazing infrastructure for Online Learning.

These places can become hybrid locations for lab access for interested students on a use-case and subscription basis along with other things.

The hostels can be a comfortable place for the youth to stay at while they're traveling to learn and network more in the industry. These universities and colleges can become a hub for entrepreneurs to set up new industries and support institutional investors to bring out funds and access to ACTUAL ease of doing business.

Once 80% of the staff in universities is out, the remaining 20% will thrive! But what will these remaining 80% do? Get trained! The current model doesn't incentivise training enough. Training should be equivalent to job security. This constant model will ensure that the number of useless staff members in universities decreases from 80% to 50% and slowly even lower.

In another contrast here, in today's times, it's easier to network through online modes. The world has shinked to your mobile screens if you want to do something but we're just not ready to incentivise and get the better of ourselves on this. If there are no colleges, networking won't stop. It will only increase and get better.

What it means basically is that people will work not with a particular company as their asset and under their identity, but instead work on a regular project basis independently. Companies can avail the services of individuals, but that's all they can do. The work is being done by an individual and being credited to an individual with the value the person thinks is correct. Yes, freelancing. Widespread freelancing. If you say that there's no job security in this and all, just look around. There is NO concept called job security anywhere in the world. But if you are good at what you do, you'll have money.

People have a lot of problems with taxes. People also forget that they're in a democracy. Opting for decentralized payments will eventually become the norm. The governments around the world can create as many barriers as they want, but the best practices and the most beneficial practices will surface up, it's all just a matter of time. This will in-turn create a more open market in the real terms. Basically, it's a capitalistic utopia. With its flaws, of course. And honestly, this isn't a new concept either. I'm just reflecting and expressing my thoughts here.

The success of individuals who have thrived without traditional college degrees further underscores the shift towards a skills-first approach. High-profile entrepreneurs like Steve Jobs, Bill Gates, and Mark Zuckerberg are often cited as examples of how passion, innovation, and practical skills can lead to success without the need for a formal education.

While these examples are extraordinary, they highlight a broader trend where skills, creativity, and experience are increasingly valued over academic qualifications. In India, too, there are numerous examples of successful professionals who have built thriving careers without a conventional degree. Many tech entrepreneurs, digital marketers, and creative professionals have leveraged their skills and experience to create successful businesses, often starting with little more than a passion for their craft and a willingness to learn.

The Indian education system, a complex network of policies, institutions, and practices, has long been considered a cornerstone of the nation's socio-economic development. However, despite its critical role in shaping the future of millions, the system remains fraught with challenges that hinder its effectiveness. These challenges stem from deep-rooted structural issues, socio-economic disparities, and a curriculum that often fails to keep pace with the evolving demands of the 21st century.

The diminishing value of college degrees has profound implications for students and graduates, many of whom find themselves disillusioned and unprepared for the realities of the job market.

The oversupply of graduates, combined with the disconnect between academia and industry, has led to a significant rise in graduate unemployment and underemployment. Many degree holders struggle to find jobs that match their qualifications, leading to a growing number of graduates who are either unemployed or working in low-paying, low-skill jobs that do not utilize their education.

This situation is particularly acute in fields like engineering, where thousands of graduates enter the job market each year, only to find that their skills are not in demand. The result is a generation of young people who are increasingly frustrated, disillusioned, and questioning the value of their education.

The financial burden of obtaining a college degree is another significant concern. The cost of higher education in India has risen steadily over the years, with many students taking on substantial debt to fund their studies. However, with the declining value of degrees and the increasing difficulty in securing well-paying jobs, many graduates find themselves struggling to repay their student loans.

This financial strain is compounded by the reality that many graduates are underemployed, working in jobs that do not provide the income needed to support themselves and repay their debts. The result is a growing crisis of student debt, with long-term implications for individuals and the economy as a whole.

Beyond the financial and professional challenges, college degrees also take an emotional toll on students and graduates. Many young people enter college with high hopes and expectations, only to find that their degrees do not lead to the opportunities they envisioned. This disillusionment can lead to a lack of direction, as graduates struggle to find their place in a job market that increasingly values skills over formal education.

This sense of disillusionment is further exacerbated by the pressure to succeed in a highly competitive environment. Many students feel overwhelmed by the demands of the education system, leading to burnout, stress, and mental health issues. The result is a generation of graduates who are not only unprepared for the job market but also emotionally and mentally drained.

And also, it's not just the academia which needs to take a hit here.

Industry is also accountable here.

By recognizing and valuing alternative credentials, employers need to ensure that they are hiring candidates who have the skills and experience needed to succeed in the modern workplace.

The diminishing value of college degrees and the shift towards a skills-first approach in the job market present both challenges and opportunities for India's education system. To ensure that our education system remains relevant and effective in preparing students for the future, it is essential to embrace change and take a proactive approach to educational reform.

Educational institutions must take the lead in rethinking their approach to higher education. This involves updating curricula, incorporating practical skills and experience, and offering flexible learning pathways that cater to the diverse needs of students. By evolving to meet the needs of the modern world, colleges can ensure that they remain relevant and effective in preparing students for the challenges of the future. Basically anything to not force feed words into the mouths of the youth to parrot them out for a piece of paper and a stamp.

Employers have a critical role to play in supporting educational reform. By prioritising skills and experience over formal degrees in their hiring practices, employers can encourage a shift towards a more skills-based approach to education. Additionally, employers can support continuous education and upskilling by offering training programs and supporting employees in their pursuit of further education.

Finally, students and parents must be open to considering alternative pathways to success. While a traditional college degree may still be the right choice for some, it is essential to recognize that there are many other ways to acquire the skills and experience needed for a successful career. By embracing alternative education pathways, students can ensure that they are well-prepared for the demands of the modern job market.

All I'll say to all parents is, if you had hard times, they made you strong people. Stop trying to create excessively good times for your children because good times make weak individuals. Let them struggle on their levels. JEE can be cracked without coaching. NEET can be cracked without coaching. Financial Stability can be achieved without a piece of paper if it's coming at the cost of livelihood.

The redundancy of traditional college degrees is a pressing issue that requires urgent attention. As the job market shifts towards a skills-first approach, it is essential to rethink our approach to education and embrace change. By promoting a more flexible, skills-based, and lifelong approach to learning, we can ensure that our education system remains relevant and effective in preparing students for the challenges of the future. The time for educational reform is now, and it is up to all of us—educational institutions, employers, government, and individuals—to take action and build a brighter future for India's youth.

The origins of the modern Indian education system can be traced back to the colonial era, where the primary objective was to create a class of clerks and subordinates to serve the British administration. This legacy has left an indelible mark on the education system, one that prioritizes conformity, rote learning, and examination success over creativity, critical thinking, and holistic development. Although independent India has made significant strides in expanding access to education, the system remains deeply flawed, failing to fully equip students with the skills and knowledge needed to thrive in a rapidly changing world.

Now, moving towards a more generalised aspect of things:

One of the most significant structural issues within the Indian education system is its highly standardized curriculum. Designed with a one-size-fits-all approach, the curriculum often lacks relevance to the diverse cultural, social, and economic contexts across the country. This homogeneity not only fails to address the unique needs of different regions and communities but also alienates students whose backgrounds and experiences do not align with the dominant narrative presented in textbooks.

The emphasis on a uniform curriculum across the nation disregards the rich diversity of languages, cultures, and traditions that exist within India. For instance, students in rural areas, where local languages and dialects are predominant, often struggle with a curriculum that is heavily oriented towards English or Hindi. This linguistic barrier creates significant challenges in comprehension and engagement, leading to higher dropout rates and lower academic performance.

Moreover, the standardized curriculum places undue emphasis on certain subjects, particularly those that are perceived to be more 'prestigious' or lucrative, such as mathematics and science, while neglecting others like the arts, humanities, and vocational training. This narrow focus not only limits students' exposure to a broad spectrum of knowledge and skills but also reinforces a rigid hierarchy of subjects that undermines the holistic development of individuals.

The Indian education system is notoriously exam-centric, with a strong emphasis on rote learning and memorization. This approach prioritizes the ability to recall information over the development of critical thinking, problem-solving, and analytical skills. As a result, students are often trained to excel in standardized tests and board exams, rather than to understand and apply concepts in real-world situations.

This obsession with examinations creates a highly competitive environment, where the pressure to perform well in exams overshadows the true purpose of education. The focus on grades and rankings leads to a culture of fear and anxiety among students, many of whom resort to rote memorization as a survival mechanism. This method of learning, however, is fundamentally flawed, as it discourages curiosity, creativity, and independent thought.

The exam-centric system also contributes to the devaluation of subjects that are not traditionally associated with high-stakes testing. Subjects like physical education, arts, and moral science are often sidelined, despite their importance in fostering well-rounded individuals. Furthermore, the relentless focus on examinations leads to a narrow definition of success, where academic achievement is measured solely by test scores, rather than by the ability to think critically, solve problems, or contribute meaningfully to society.

Another critical issue within the Indian education system is the prevalence of teacher-centric pedagogy, where the teacher is the sole authority in the classroom, and students are passive recipients of information. This traditional model of education limits student engagement and stifles active participation, reducing learning to a unidirectional transfer of knowledge.

In many classrooms, especially in government schools, the pedagogical approach is characterized by long lectures, where teachers read from textbooks or dictate notes, while students listen passively. This method not only fails to engage students but also reinforces a culture of dependency, where students rely on teachers for knowledge, rather than actively seeking out information and learning on their own.

Moreover, the lack of interactive and experiential learning opportunities means that students are often unable to connect theoretical knowledge with practical applications. This disconnect between classroom learning and real-world experiences contributes to the perception that education is irrelevant or disconnected from everyday life.

The problem is further exacerbated by the inadequate training and professional development opportunities available to teachers. Many teachers, especially in rural areas, lack the necessary skills and resources to adopt more student-centered and innovative teaching methods. Without ongoing support and training, teachers are often unable to create a dynamic and engaging learning environment that encourages student participation and fosters critical thinking.

Despite the significant expansion of the education system in India over the past few decades, access to quality education remains deeply unequal. Socio-economic disparities, particularly between urban and rural areas, create significant barriers to education for millions of children. While urban students often have access to well-equipped schools, qualified teachers, and a broad range of educational resources, their rural counterparts struggle with inadequate infrastructure, poorly trained teachers, and a lack of basic educational materials.

The urban-rural divide is particularly stark when it comes to access to secondary and higher education. In many rural areas, secondary schools are few and far between, forcing students to travel long distances or drop out altogether. This lack of access to higher levels of education perpetuates a cycle of poverty and marginalization, as students from rural areas are often unable to compete with their urban peers in the job market.

Gender disparities further exacerbate the issue of access and equity in the Indian education system. Despite significant progress in recent years, girls continue to face significant barriers to education, particularly in rural areas. Cultural norms and gender biases often prioritize the education of boys over girls, leading to higher dropout rates among female students. Early marriage, domestic responsibilities, and safety concerns also contribute to the lower participation of girls in secondary and higher education.

The inadequate infrastructure and lack of resources in many Indian schools pose significant challenges to the delivery of quality education. This issue is particularly acute in government schools, which serve the majority of the country's children, especially in rural and economically disadvantaged areas.

Many schools lack basic facilities such as clean drinking water, functional toilets, and adequate classrooms. In some cases, students are forced to study in overcrowded and poorly ventilated classrooms, with little access to libraries, laboratories, or playgrounds. The lack of proper infrastructure not only affects the physical well-being of students but also hampers their ability to learn effectively.

The digital divide is another significant barrier to quality education in India. While urban students often have access to computers, the internet, and other digital resources, their rural counterparts are largely excluded from the benefits of digital learning. This gap has become even more pronounced in the wake of the COVID-19 pandemic, where the shift to online education has highlighted the stark disparities in access to technology.

In addition to the lack of physical infrastructure, many schools also suffer from a shortage of qualified teachers and educational materials. In rural areas, teachers are often underqualified, overburdened, and poorly trained, leading to substandard teaching and poor learning outcomes. The lack of textbooks, teaching aids, and other learning materials further compounds the problem, leaving students with few opportunities to engage with the curriculum in meaningful ways.

The rapid growth of private schools and coaching centers in India has created a parallel education system that exacerbates existing inequalities. While private schools often offer better infrastructure, qualified teachers, and a broader range of extracurricular activities, they are also prohibitively expensive for many families, particularly those from lower-income backgrounds.

The commercialization of education has led to a situation where access to quality education is increasingly determined by one's ability to pay. This trend is particularly evident in the proliferation of coaching centers that prepare students for competitive exams such as the Joint Entrance Examination (JEE) and the National Eligibility cum Entrance Test (NEET). These centers charge exorbitant fees, creating a significant financial burden for families and reinforcing the divide between those who can afford private coaching and those who cannot.

The privatization of education also raises concerns about the commodification of learning, where education is treated as a product to be bought and sold, rather than a fundamental right. This shift in perspective undermines the broader social and developmental goals of education, as it prioritizes individual success over collective well-being and equity.

The curriculum in many Indian schools remains outdated and disconnected from the realities of the 21st-century job market. While the world around us is changing rapidly, with new technologies and industries emerging, the education system has been slow to adapt. As a result, students are often taught content that is no longer relevant or applicable to their future careers.

For instance, while the importance of STEM (science, technology, engineering, and mathematics) education is widely recognized, the curriculum often fails to go beyond theoretical knowledge, leaving students unprepared for practical applications in the workforce. At the same time, there is a glaring lack of emphasis on vocational training, entrepreneurship, and life skills, all of which are essential for success in today's economy.

Moreover, the curriculum often overlooks critical areas such as environmental education, mental health, and civic duties. In a world facing unprecedented environmental challenges, it is crucial that students are equipped with

 the knowledge and skills to address issues like climate change and sustainability. Similarly, the growing mental health crisis among young people underscores the need for education systems to prioritize emotional well-being and provide students with the tools to navigate the complexities of modern life.

The Indian education system has been criticized for its tendency to promote cultural homogenization, where regional languages, traditions, and histories are marginalized in favor of a more uniform national narrative. This approach not only undermines the rich diversity of the country but also alienates students whose cultural backgrounds are not adequately represented in the curriculum.

For example, while Hindi and English are often prioritized in the curriculum, regional languages and dialects are neglected, leading to a loss of linguistic diversity and cultural identity. This linguistic marginalization has significant implications for students' ability to connect with their heritage and feel a sense of belonging within the education system.

Furthermore, the curriculum often fails to adequately represent the histories and contributions of minority communities, reinforcing dominant narratives that overlook the experiences and struggles of marginalized groups. This lack of representation not only perpetuates social inequalities but also limits students' understanding of the diverse and complex history of their country.

The Indian education system's over-prioritization of STEM subjects at the expense of the humanities and social sciences has long-term implications for the holistic development of students. While STEM education is undeniably important in a technology-driven world, the humanities play a crucial role in fostering critical thinking, empathy, and a deeper understanding of human experiences.

The emphasis on STEM subjects often leads to the neglect of subjects like literature, history, philosophy, and the arts, which are essential for developing well-rounded individuals capable of thinking critically about the world around them. This narrow focus on technical education also limits students' exposure to diverse perspectives and ways of thinking, which are necessary for addressing complex social, ethical, and cultural issues.

Moreover, the devaluation of the humanities contributes to a societal perception that these subjects are less valuable or less likely to lead to successful careers. This perception discourages students from pursuing their passions in the humanities and reinforces a rigid hierarchy of disciplines that undermines the broader goals of education.

One of the most significant challenges facing the Indian education system is the gap between policy intent and ground reality. While the government has introduced several policies and initiatives aimed at improving the quality of education, these efforts often fall short in their implementation due to bureaucratic inefficiencies, corruption, and a lack of accountability.

For instance, the Right to Education (RTE) Act, which guarantees free and compulsory education for all children aged 6 to 14, has been hailed as a landmark achievement in ensuring access to education. However, the implementation of the RTE Act has been plagued by challenges, including inadequate funding, a shortage of trained teachers, and poor monitoring and evaluation mechanisms.

Similarly, initiatives aimed at improving the quality of education, such as the introduction of Continuous and Comprehensive Evaluation (CCE) and the mid-day meal scheme, have faced significant hurdles in their implementation. In many cases, these initiatives have failed to achieve their intended outcomes due to a lack of coordination between different levels of government, insufficient resources, and weak enforcement mechanisms.

The National Education Policy (NEP) 2020 has been widely regarded as a transformative step towards reforming the Indian education system. The policy outlines several ambitious goals, including the introduction of multidisciplinary education, the integration of vocational training, and the promotion of experiential and holistic learning.

However, while the NEP 2020 presents a promising vision for the future of education in India, its success will ultimately depend on its implementation. The policy's ambitious goals will require significant investments in infrastructure, teacher training, and curriculum development, as well as strong political will and effective governance.

Critics of the NEP 2020 have also raised concerns about its potential to exacerbate existing inequalities in the education system. For instance, the policy's emphasis on digital learning and online education could further widen the digital divide between urban and rural students. Similarly, the policy's focus on multidisciplinary education may be challenging to implement in government schools, where resources and infrastructure are already stretched thin.

The debate over central control versus local autonomy in education is a longstanding one in India. On the one hand, centralization allows for greater uniformity and standardization across the country, ensuring that all students receive a similar quality of education. On the other hand, decentralization allows for greater flexibility and responsiveness to local needs and contexts, enabling schools to tailor their curricula and teaching methods to the unique needs of their students.

In recent years, there has been a growing recognition of the importance of decentralization in education, with several states experimenting with decentralized models of school management and curriculum design. These models have shown promising results in improving student outcomes and increasing community involvement in education.

However, the move towards decentralization also presents challenges, particularly in terms of ensuring consistency and accountability across the education system. Without adequate support and oversight from central authorities, there is a risk that decentralized models could lead to disparities in the quality of education between different regions and communities.

The intense pressure to perform well in exams and secure high grades has a significant impact on the mental health and well-being of students in India. The education system's relentless focus on academic achievement creates a culture of stress and anxiety, where students are constantly under pressure to meet unrealistic expectations.

This pressure is particularly acute during high-stakes exams such as the board exams and competitive entrance tests, where the outcome can have a profound impact on a student's future prospects. The fear of failure and the consequences of not meeting these expectations can lead to severe anxiety, depression, and even suicidal tendencies among students.

Despite the growing recognition of the mental health crisis among students, there is a lack of adequate support and counseling services in schools. Many schools do not have trained counselors or mental health professionals who can provide the necessary support to students struggling with stress and anxiety. As a result, students are often left to cope with these challenges on their own, leading to long-term psychological and emotional consequences.

The Indian education system's emphasis on conformity and uniformity often stifles creativity and individuality, leading to a lack of motivation and passion for learning among students. The system's rigid structure and standardized curriculum leave little room for students to explore their interests, pursue their passions, or develop their unique talents.

This focus on conformity is evident in the way students are assessed and evaluated, where success is often measured by how well they conform to established norms and expectations. Students who do not fit into this mold, whether due to different learning styles, interests, or abilities, are often marginalized or labeled as 'failures'.

The lack of opportunities for self-expression and creative exploration also has a significant impact on students' sense of identity and self-worth. In a system that prioritizes academic achievement over personal growth, students are often discouraged from pursuing unconventional or non-academic paths, leading to a narrow definition of success that overlooks the diverse talents and potential of individuals.

Social conditioning and peer pressure play a significant role in shaping students' career choices and academic aspirations in India. From a young age, students are often conditioned to believe that certain careers, such as engineering, medicine, or law, are more prestigious or desirable than others. This social conditioning is reinforced by parents, teachers, and peers, leading to a narrow perception of success that is centered around these traditional professions.

The pressure to conform to these societal expectations can have a profound impact on students' choices and decisions. Many students feel compelled to pursue careers that are socially acceptable, even if they have no interest or passion for these fields. This pressure can lead to a lack of motivation, dissatisfaction, and burnout, as students are forced to follow paths that do not align with their true interests or aspirations.

Moreover, the stigma associated with unconventional career paths or non-academic pursuits further reinforces the rigid hierarchy of professions in India. Students who choose to pursue careers in the arts, sports, or other non-traditional fields are often met with skepticism or disapproval, leading to a lack of support and recognition for their achievements.

To gain a better understanding of the limitations and potential reforms for the Indian education system, it is useful to compare it with successful education models from other countries. Nations like Finland, Japan, and the United States offer valuable insights into alternative approaches to education that prioritize holistic development, equity, and adaptability.

For instance, Finland's education system is renowned for its emphasis on student well-being, personalized learning, and minimal standardized testing. In contrast to India's exam-centric approach, Finland focuses on creating a supportive and collaborative learning environment, where students are encouraged to explore their interests and develop critical thinking skills. This model has resulted in consistently high educational outcomes and strong student satisfaction.

Japan, on the other hand, places a strong emphasis on discipline, respect, and moral education, alongside academic achievement. The Japanese education system fosters a sense of community and collective responsibility, where students are taught the importance of cooperation, hard work, and social harmony. This approach has contributed to high levels of academic achievement and social cohesion in Japanese society.

The United States offers a more decentralized and flexible education system, where schools have greater autonomy to design curricula and adopt innovative teaching methods. This flexibility allows for a diverse range of educational approaches, from project-based learning to experiential education, which cater to the unique needs and interests of students. However, the US system also faces challenges related to equity and access, particularly in underserved communities.

In addition to learning from global models, it is important to recognize the innovative efforts within India to address the limitations of the mainstream education system. Several alternative education movements and initiatives have emerged in recent years, offering new approaches to learning that prioritize creativity, experiential learning, and social justice.

One such initiative is the rise of alternative schools that focus on child-centered and holistic education. These schools, such as the Krishnamurti Foundation schools, the Rishi Valley School, and the Mirambika Free Progress School, emphasize the importance of nurturing the whole child—intellectually, emotionally, and spiritually. These schools often adopt innovative teaching methods, such as project-based learning, experiential education, and arts integration, which encourage students to think critically, explore their passions, and develop a love for learning.

Another notable movement is the emergence of grassroots education initiatives in rural and marginalized communities. Organizations like Pratham, Ekal Vidyalaya, and the Barefoot College are working to provide quality education to underserved populations, using innovative and context-specific approaches. These initiatives often involve community participation, use of local languages and cultural practices, and a focus on vocational and life skills, which help bridge the gap between formal education and the realities of rural life.

These alternative education movements offer valuable insights into how the Indian education system can be reimagined to better serve the diverse needs of its students. By drawing on these examples, policymakers and educators can explore new ways of creating a more inclusive, equitable, and dynamic education system that prepares students for the challenges of the future.

One of the most critical steps in reforming the Indian education system is reimagining the curriculum to make it more relevant, inclusive, and dynamic. This involves moving away from a standardized, one-size-fits-all approach and embracing a more flexible and interdisciplinary curriculum that reflects the diverse needs and interests of students.

The curriculum should be updated to include contemporary issues such as climate change, digital literacy, and global citizenship, which are essential for preparing students for the challenges of the 21st century. Additionally, there should be a greater emphasis on vocational education, entrepreneurship, and life skills, which equip students with the practical knowledge and skills needed to succeed in a rapidly changing world.

Furthermore, the curriculum should be designed to promote critical thinking, creativity, and problem-solving, rather than rote learning and memorization. This can be achieved by incorporating more project-based learning, experiential education, and interdisciplinary studies, which encourage students to engage with real-world issues and develop a deeper understanding of the subjects they are studying.

Empowering teachers and schools is another crucial aspect of education reform in India. Teachers play a central role in shaping the learning experiences of students, and it is essential that they are provided with the necessary support, resources, and professional development opportunities to excel in their roles.

This includes investing in teacher training and continuous professional development programs that equip teachers with the skills and knowledge to adopt innovative teaching methods, create inclusive and engaging learning environments, and support the holistic development of students. Additionally, teachers should be empowered to take on leadership roles within their schools, participate in curriculum design, and contribute to the broader educational discourse.

Schools, too, should be given greater autonomy to design and implement curricula that reflect the unique needs and contexts of their students. This requires a shift towards a more decentralized education system, where schools have the flexibility to experiment with new approaches to teaching and learning, while also being held accountable for their performance and outcomes.

Ensuring that all students have access to quality education, regardless of their socio-economic background, is a fundamental goal of education reform in India. This requires addressing the deep-rooted inequalities and barriers that prevent marginalized communities from fully participating in the education system.

Policies and initiatives aimed at promoting equity and inclusion should focus on providing targeted support to disadvantaged students, such as scholarships, remedial programs, and mentorship opportunities. Additionally, there should be a concerted effort to improve the infrastructure and resources of government schools, particularly in rural and underserved areas, to ensure that all students have access to a safe and conducive learning environment.

Furthermore, the curriculum and teaching methods should be designed to reflect the diverse cultural, linguistic, and socio-economic backgrounds of students, and to promote a sense of belonging and respect for all identities. This includes incorporating local languages, traditions, and histories into the curriculum, as well as addressing issues of social justice, discrimination, and inequality within the classroom.

Finally, education reform in India should aim to foster a culture of lifelong learning, where individuals are encouraged to continue learning and developing throughout their lives. This requires a shift away from the current model of education, which is focused primarily on formal schooling, towards a more holistic and flexible approach that includes opportunities for adult education, vocational training, and informal learning.

Lifelong learning initiatives should be designed to cater to the needs of all individuals, regardless of their age, gender, or socio-economic background. This includes providing access to affordable and flexible learning opportunities, such as online courses, community-based education programs, and workplace training, which allow individuals to acquire new skills and knowledge at any stage of their lives.

Moreover, there should be a greater emphasis on developing a learning culture within society, where education is valued as a lifelong pursuit, rather than a means to an end. This can be achieved by promoting the importance of continuous learning through public awareness campaigns, community initiatives, and policy frameworks that support and incentivize lifelong learning.

The Indian education system stands at a crossroads, with the opportunity to redefine its approach to learning and development for future generations. By addressing the constraints and limitations that have long plagued the system, and embracing new and innovative approaches to education, India can create a more holistic, inclusive, and dynamic education system that prepares students to thrive in an increasingly complex and interconnected world.

The path to reform is not without its challenges, but with a concerted effort from policymakers, educators, and communities, it is possible to create an education system that reflects the diverse needs and aspirations of India's youth, and that contributes to the broader goals of social and economic development.

As we look to the future, it is essential that we continue to question and challenge the status quo, and to explore new ways of thinking about education that go beyond traditional models and paradigms. By doing so, we can create a more equitable, empowering, and transformative education system that truly reflects the potential of every individual, and that helps to build a more just and sustainable society for all.

The Alchemist

Stepping back into his room was like inhaling a breath of fresh air after a long, suffocating dive. The familiar scent of sandalwood incense, the soft glow of the bedside lamp, the comforting weight of his well-worn blanket - it all enveloped Parth in a cocoon of warmth and security. He sank into his bed, his gaze tracing the familiar contours of his room, his heart swelling with gratitude for the simple comforts he had once taken for granted.

Mohini was the first to visit, a glass of freshly squeezed orange juice in her hand. She perched on the edge of his bed,her eyes filled with a mix of concern and affection.

"How are you feeling, Parth?" she asked softly, her voice a soothing balm to his frayed nerves.

Parth managed a weak smile. "Better, now that I'm home."

They fell into a comfortable silence, the only sound the gentle clinking of ice cubes against the glass. Then, Mohini spoke, her voice laced with a newfound understanding.

"You know, Parth," she began, her gaze distant, "I've been thinking a lot about our conversation in the hospital."

Parth nodded, his heart heavy with unspoken words.

"I realized that we're both victims of the same system, and somehow, me clearing JEE with an astounding score and getting excellent scores and all, it created unnecessary pressure on you" Mohini continued. "Sadly, we are in a system that tells us what to study, what to aspire

to, but never teaches us how to truly live. It's no wonder we feel lost and confused."

Her words resonated with Parth, a painful truth echoing through his mind. He had always felt like a square peg trying to fit into a round hole, his passions and dreams at odds with the expectations of the world around him.

Mohini reached out, her hand gently squeezing his. "But we don't have to let the system define us, Parth. We can forge our own paths, find our own purpose, even within its limitations. It's okay if you want to do something else. Explore whatever you want to do. I'm always with you."

Her words ignited a flicker of hope in Parth's heart. Perhaps it wasn't too late. Perhaps he could still find his way, even after all the setbacks and failures.

"I have thought of painting, you know", Parth said with a faint smile.

Mohini squeezed her eyes, "You don't have to test me the second I say that I'm always with you. Cause the last drawing you made, even the sun wasn't a circle!"

While they both laughed, their mother entered the room, a steaming bowl of khichdi in her hands. Parth wrinkled his nose playfully. "Khichdi again, Ma?" Mohini laughed and exited the room to get herself something to eat

His mother chuckled, her eyes sparkling with love. "It's good for you, beta. And besides," she added with a wink, "it's better than anything you got in that hospital, right?"

Parth laughed, a genuine sound that surprised even himself. As he ate, the conversation turned to his struggles, his regrets, his perceived failures. His mother listened patiently, her hand resting on his arm, a silent source of strength. "I am not as good as Di. She contributes in so many ways. I am nothing but a load to you and Pa."

"Parth," she said softly, her voice thick with emotion, *"you are so much more than your achievements. You are kind, compassionate, and intelligent. I didn't raise you to become an engineer, neither did your father. You are our son. That's how we raised you. As an individual who can keep fighting through endless odds without giving up. And we love you unconditionally for that."*

Tears welled up in Parth's eyes. "But I've let you down, Ma. I've failed you."

His mother shook her head, her gaze unwavering. "You have never been a failure in our eyes, beta. You are our pride and joy, and we will always be here for you, no matter what."

After a good afternoon nap, Ashwini entered the room, a sombre expression on his face. He placed a tray of medicines on the bedside table and sat down beside Parth. For a long moment, they sat in silence, the weight of unspoken words hanging heavy in the air.

Finally, his father broke the silence. "Why were you on that road?"

Parth's breath hitched in his throat. He couldn't see his father's eyes.

"I know you were drunk," his father continued, his voice gentle but firm. "And I know you were driving."

Parth's composure crumbled. Tears streamed down his face as he buried his head in his hands. "I'm so sorry, Papa," he was almost sobbing. "I didn't know what I was doing. I just... I wanted it all to end."

His father's hand rested on his shoulder, a comforting weight. "Why, Parth? Why did you feel that way?"

A sob escaped his lips, and he continued, his voice trembling, "I... I had been drinking with some friends. I shouldn't have... but I did. And then, I borrowed someone's Activa to go back to the hostel. On the flyover, everything just... overwhelmed me. The thoughts wouldn't stop. I felt so useless, so pointless..."

He paused, his breath hitching in his throat. "I thought about ending it all, Papa. Right there, on that flyover."

His father's grip tightened on his shoulder. "Oh, Parth..."

"Just as I was about to... to do something stupid, I saw a bus speeding towards me. I swerved, trying to avoid it... and I did. But then... I lost control. I went over to the wrong side of the road..."

Parth's voice trailed off, the memory of the impact too painful to recount.

His father's face was etched with sorrow and understanding. "The police told us you were thrown from the flyover. You landed almost two kilometers away, near the bus stop that fell on the other side. The impact... It was severe. The engine fell on your face, your arm..."

Parth's voice was barely a whisper. "I felt like a failure, Papa. I couldn't live up to your expectations. I felt like I was a burden on you, that you were disappointed in me."

His father's eyes softened, but his voice had absolute resolve and assertion. "Parth"

Parth hesitantly raised his head, his vision blurred by tears.

"I am nothing but proud of you," his father said, his voice filled with unwavering love.

Parth collapsed into his father's arms, his sobs wracking his body. The words he was dying to hear from him father's mouth. The words for which he would be ready to take a bullet. The only thing he aspired to get. All of it felt like a cheat. Like he didn't deserve it. Like he wanted to hear it not in such a time. But, nevertheless, there was no thought left as his father held him close, Parth felt a sense of peace he hadn't experienced in a long time. He knew that he had a long road to recovery ahead of him, both physically and emotionally. But with the love and support of his family, he was determined to find his way back to the light.

Although, of course, he knew, there's a long way to go. He still has to figure out what he wants to do and how…

Picture a young student, eyes filled with dreams and aspirations, stepping into the vast and intricate labyrinth of India's education system. This student, much like the alchemist of Paulo Coelho's renowned novel, embarks on a transformative journey. Like the alchemist who seeks to transmute base metals into gold, the student navigates the challenging and often hostile terrain of the Indian education system, striving to extract knowledge, wisdom, and personal growth from its crucible. This chapter delves deep into the trials and triumphs of this alchemical journey,offering guidance to students, parents, educators, and institutions alike.

In the heart of India's bustling education landscape, a student embarks on a transformative journey akin to that of an alchemist. Like the alchemist who strives to transmute base metals into gold, the student navigates the challenging and often hostile terrain of the Indian education system, seeking to extract knowledge, wisdom, and personal growth from its crucible. This chapter delves deep into the trials and triumphs of this alchemical journey, offering guidance to students, parents, educators, and institutions alike on how to navigate and improve this system.

The Indian education system, a tapestry woven with threads of rich history and cultural significance, is a complex and multifaceted entity. It is a system that has produced brilliant minds, groundbreaking innovations, and countless success stories. However, it is also a system fraught with challenges, inequities, and rigid structures that can often hinder the holistic development of its students. Let's embark on a journey through the various stages of this system, exploring the hurdles and opportunities that students encounter along the way.

The formative years of primary education lay the groundwork for a child's intellectual, social, and emotional development. It is during this stage that children develop a love for learning, acquire foundational skills, and begin to explore their interests and talents. However, for many children in India, especially those from marginalized communities and rural areas, accessing quality primary education remains a distant dream. The challenges they face are multifaceted and deeply ingrained in the socio-economic fabric of the nation.

The lack of adequate infrastructure, particularly in rural and remote areas, is a major obstacle to primary education.Overcrowded classrooms, dilapidated buildings, and a shortage of qualified teachers create a challenging learning environment that can severely impede a child's progress. Moreover, the long distances to schools and the lack of safe transportation options can further deter children from attending school regularly, particularly girls and children with disabilities. This creates a significant barrier to education, limiting opportunities and perpetuating the cycle of poverty and inequality.

The issue of accessibility is further compounded by socio-cultural factors. In many communities, there is a lack of awareness about the importance of education, especially for girls. Early marriage, child labor, and gender discrimination can all contribute to low enrollment and high dropout rates, particularly among girls. Addressing these deep-rooted social issues is crucial to ensuring that every child, regardless of their background, has the opportunity to access quality education.

Even when schools are accessible, the quality of education often leaves much to be desired. The traditional emphasis on rote learning and memorization, coupled with a lack of engaging teaching methods and resources, can stifle creativity,critical thinking, and problem-solving skills. The pressure to perform well in exams from a young age can also lead to anxiety and stress, robbing children of the joy of learning and hindering their holistic development.

The lack of qualified and motivated teachers is a major contributor to the quality gap in primary education. Many teachers, especially in government schools, are underpaid, overworked, and lack adequate training and support. This can lead to a demotivated and disengaged teaching force, further impacting the quality of education. Moreover, the curriculum in many schools is often outdated and irrelevant, failing to equip students with the skills they need to succeed in the 21st century.

In a small village nestled in the foothills of the Himalayas, the local primary school paints a poignant picture of the challenges faced by rural education in India. The school building, though functional, is in a state of disrepair, with cracked walls, broken windows, and inadequate sanitation facilities. The classrooms are overcrowded, with children of different ages and abilities crammed together, making it difficult for teachers to provide individualized attention.

The school has only two teachers, both of whom are overburdened with administrative tasks and struggle to keep up with the demands of the curriculum. The lack of teaching aids, such as textbooks, charts, and interactive learning materials, further hampers their ability to deliver effective instruction. The children, many of whom come from poor families and face malnutrition, struggle to concentrate and often fall behind in their studies.

The school also grapples with issues of absenteeism and dropout rates, particularly among girls. Early marriage, child labor, and the need to help their families with household chores or farm work often force girls to leave school prematurely. The lack of awareness about the importance of education, coupled with the perception that education is a luxury rather than a necessity, further contributes to this problem.

Addressing the challenges in primary education requires a multi-pronged and sustained effort that involves increased investment in infrastructure, teacher training, curriculum reform, and community engagement.

First of all, the government needs to prioritize the construction of new schools and the renovation of existing ones, particularly in rural and underserved areas. Ensuring that schools have adequate classrooms, libraries, laboratories, sanitation facilities, and playgrounds is crucial for creating a conducive and inclusive learning environment. The privileged students from the top 10% families shouldn't be seen as a successful metric for the system to succeed.

Every child deserves the right to education, with emphasis on education, and not literacy. Today, the system focuses on literacy over education which in turn creates great mediocre employees for medium and small enterprises, but the country won't be able to produce the next olympics gold medalist, or the next MS Dhoni, or even the next Vikram Sarabhai without showing the children where education, in whatever field they're interested in, can take them.

Secondly, Teachers are the cornerstone of the education system. Investing in their training and development is essential to improve the quality of teaching and learning. Providing teachers with ongoing professional development opportunities, access to modern teaching resources, and a supportive work environment can empower them to deliver effective and engaging instruction that caters to the diverse needs of their students.

The knowledge and skills of the subject matter requires to be inquisitively questionable. Every teacher I remember today, I remember them for being extremely patient to a student like me, someone who was pretty much hated by most of my peers for asking too many questions in the middle of the class disrupting and disturbing the flow. I am ever grateful for them as they understand how a classroom doesn't need to be a lecture but rather a conversation.

Not everyone is that fortunate, though. Teaching needs to become a profession of great pride as it's a noble profession, which is not at all rewarding for the masses.

Next, the curriculum needs to be revamped to focus on conceptual understanding, critical thinking, problem-solving, and communication skills. Incorporating experiential learning, project-based activities, and technology can make learning more interactive, relevant, and enjoyable. The curriculum should also be culturally sensitive and inclusive, reflecting the diversity of India's population.

Engaging parents and the community in the education process is crucial for ensuring that children receive the support and encouragement they need to succeed. Creating awareness about the importance of education, promoting parental involvement in school activities, and leveraging community resources can contribute to a more holistic and effective learning experience.

Most importantly, tackling deep-rooted social issues such as child marriage, child labor, and gender discrimination is essential for ensuring that all children have equal access to education. Awareness campaigns, community mobilization efforts, and strict enforcement of laws against child labor and early marriage can help create a more conducive environment for education.

Education about gender, races and various aspects of society, matched with proper sexual education at early classes can be a good way, and probably the only way for our country to actually reduce our rape rates.

Primary education is the foundation upon which a child's future is built. By addressing the challenges and investing in quality primary education, we can empower children to reach their full potential and contribute to the nation's progress.The journey towards a more equitable and effective primary education system is a long one, but it is a journey that we must embark on with determination and resolve. The future of India's children depends on it.

As students transition from primary to secondary education, they step onto a path filled with choices and challenges that will profoundly shape their academic and career trajectories. This phase is a pivotal juncture where intellectual curiosity meets societal expectations, and individual aspirations clash with the pressure to conform. It's a period of immense growth and self-discovery, but also one fraught with potential pitfalls.

The sheer number of subject choices and career paths can be overwhelming for students at the secondary level. The pressure to choose the "right" stream – science, commerce, or humanities – can lead to anxiety and confusion. This decision is often heavily influenced by societal expectations, parental aspirations, and the perceived prestige and earning potential associated with certain fields.

The science stream, with its promise of lucrative careers in engineering and medicine, often reigns supreme in the hierarchy of choices. However, this narrow focus on science and technology can lead to the neglect of other equally important disciplines, such as humanities, arts, and social sciences. The arts, often dismissed as "unconventional" or "non-serious," are relegated to the sidelines, depriving students of the opportunity to explore their creativity, critical thinking, and communication skills.

This skewed preference for science and commerce streams can create a lopsided education system that fails to nurture the diverse talents and interests of students. It can lead to a generation of individuals who excel in technical skills but lack the well-roundedness and adaptability required to thrive in the 21st century. It is imperative to create an education system that values and encourages all streams equally, allowing students to pursue their passions and develop their unique talents.

Most importantly, awareness towards alternative careers needs to be a clear thing. My best friends are in the biotechnology field and they're doing great. The scope and growth in biotechnology shows so much promise. Most of them, at some point, wanted to become doctors or wanted to get into pharmaceuticals.

How many nano-scientists have you seen? How many material scientists do you know? Do you know anyone who is working on vaccines? Do you someone who's working on sustainable infrastructure?

The intense competition for admission to top colleges and universities has spawned a thriving coaching industry in India. It's a rat-race and hence, easy and convenient. We don't want the discomfort of having independent thought, and hence, just keep walking, praying to lord that maybe, hopefully, we end up in a place where what we want to actually do automatically comes in front of us.

Students, driven by the desire to secure a coveted seat in their dream institution, spend countless hours after school attending coaching classes, often sacrificing their health, well-being, and overall development.

While coaching classes can provide valuable academic support and guidance, they also perpetuate a culture of rote learning, exam-centricity, and unhealthy competition. The pressure to perform well in both school and coaching classes can lead to stress, burnout, and a loss of interest in learning for its own sake. The focus on memorization and regurgitation of information leaves little room for creativity, critical thinking, and the development of essential life skills.

Moreover, the high cost of coaching classes can create a financial burden for families, further exacerbating educational inequities. Students from low-income backgrounds may be unable to afford these additional classes, putting them at a significant disadvantage in the competitive race for college admissions. This creates a system where access to quality education is increasingly determined by financial resources, rather than merit or potential.

The increasing reliance on technology in education has created a digital divide, where students from affluent backgrounds have access to computers, internet connectivity, and online learning resources, while those from marginalized communities are left behind. This digital divide can severely limit educational opportunities and perpetuate existing inequalities.

The COVID-19 pandemic, with its forced shift to online learning, has further exposed the stark reality of the digital divide. Students from low-income families, particularly in rural areas, struggled to access online classes due to a lack of devices and internet connectivity. This resulted in learning losses and widened the achievement gap between privileged and disadvantaged students, highlighting the urgent need to bridge the digital divide to ensure equitable access to education for all.

The digital divide is not just about access to devices and connectivity; it's also about digital literacy and the ability to use technology effectively for learning. Many students from marginalized communities lack the skills and knowledge to navigate online platforms, access educational resources, and participate in virtual classrooms. This creates another layer of disadvantage that needs to be addressed through targeted digital literacy programs and training.

The pressures of secondary education extend beyond academics. The constant competition, societal expectations, and the fear of failure can take a toll on the mental and emotional well-being of students. Anxiety, depression, and other mental health issues are alarmingly prevalent among adolescents, often stemming from the stress and pressures they face in their academic lives.

The stigma surrounding mental health in India often prevents students from seeking help or even acknowledging their struggles. This can lead to a downward spiral, where untreated mental health issues can further impact their academic performance, social relationships, and overall quality of life. It is crucial to create a supportive and inclusive school environment where students feel comfortable talking about their mental health and seeking help without fear of judgment or discrimination.

Addressing the challenges in secondary education requires a paradigm shift that moves away from rote learning and exam-centric approaches towards a more holistic and student-centric model. This transformation involves a multi-faceted approach that encompasses curriculum reform, assessment methods, digital inclusion, mental health support,and career guidance.

By reimagining the curriculum, transforming assessment methods, bridging the digital divide, addressing the coaching culture, providing career guidance and counseling, and prioritizing mental health, we can create a secondary education system that empowers students to thrive academically, emotionally, and socially. This will not only prepare them for the challenges of the 21st century but also enable them to lead fulfilling and purposeful lives. The journey towards a more equitable, inclusive, and empowering secondary education system is a collective responsibility that requires the commitment of educators, policymakers, parents, and society at large. It is a journey that will shape the future of India's youth and, ultimately, the nation itself.

As students emerge from the crucible of secondary education, they step onto the threshold of higher studies, a phase brimming with possibilities and aspirations. This is where their academic journey culminates, where they delve deeper into their chosen fields, refine their skills, and prepare to embark on their professional careers. Yet, the path to higher education in India is not without its challenges. It's a landscape marked by limited access, financial barriers, concerns about quality, and a growing disconnect between academia and industry. Let's explore these challenges in detail and contemplate potential solutions to create a more equitable and empowering higher education system.

The pursuit of higher education, particularly in professional courses like engineering, medicine, and management, often comes with a hefty price tag. The high cost of tuition fees, hostel charges, and other associated expenses can be a major deterrent for students from low-income families. The dream of attending a prestigious university or pursuing a specialized course often remains a distant reality for those who cannot afford the financial burden.

While scholarships and financial aid programs exist, they are often limited in number and highly competitive, leaving many deserving students unable to access the education they need to realize their potential. This creates a system where access to higher education is increasingly determined by financial resources, rather than merit or potential, perpetuating a cycle of inequality and limiting social mobility.

Moreover, the rising cost of living in major cities, where many top-tier institutions are located, adds another layer of financial strain. Students from rural areas or small towns often struggle to cope with the high costs of accommodation,food, and transportation. This can force them to compromise on their living conditions or take up part-time jobs, which can further impact their academic performance and overall well-being.

To address the affordability barrier, a multi-pronged approach is needed. This includes increasing government funding for higher education, expanding scholarship and financial aid programs, and exploring innovative financing models such as income-share agreements. Institutions can also play a role by offering flexible payment plans, reducing non-essential fees, and providing on-campus work opportunities for students from low-income backgrounds.

While India boasts of some world-renowned universities and institutions, the overall quality of higher education remains uneven. Many colleges and universities, especially in the private sector, are plagued by a range of issues that impact the learning experience and career prospects of students.

One of the major concerns is the outdated and rigid curriculum that often fails to keep pace with the rapidly changing demands of the job market. The emphasis on theoretical knowledge over practical skills, the lack of industry exposure,and the limited opportunities for research and innovation can leave graduates ill-equipped to face the challenges of the 21st-century workplace.

Another critical issue is the shortage of qualified and experienced faculty. Many institutions, particularly in Tier 2 and Tier 3 cities, struggle to attract and retain talented faculty due to low salaries, limited research opportunities, and a lack of professional development avenues. This can compromise the quality of teaching and mentorship, hindering students' learning and growth.

Furthermore, inadequate infrastructure, including outdated laboratories, libraries, and classrooms, can create a suboptimal learning environment. The lack of access to modern technology and resources can further limit students' exposure to cutting-edge research and innovation.

To enhance the quality of higher education, a comprehensive approach is needed. This includes revamping curricula to focus on practical skills, industry-relevant knowledge, and interdisciplinary learning. Investing in faculty development,promoting research and innovation, and upgrading infrastructure are also crucial steps towards creating a more stimulating and enriching learning environment.

The disconnect between the skills imparted in higher education and the demands of the job market is a growing concern. Many graduates, despite their degrees and diplomas, lack the practical skills, industry knowledge, and soft skills required to succeed in the workplace. This skill gap not only leads to unemployment and underemployment but also hampers the nation's economic growth and competitiveness.

Bridging this skill gap requires a collaborative effort between educational institutions, industry, and the government.Institutions need to revamp their curricula to focus on practical skills, industry-relevant knowledge, and soft skills such as communication, teamwork, and problem-solving. Industry-academia partnerships, internships, and apprenticeships can provide students with valuable hands-on experience and exposure to the workplace, enabling them to develop the skills and knowledge that employers seek.

The government can play a crucial role in promoting skill development and creating a more conducive environment for industry-academia collaboration. Initiatives such as the National Skill Development Mission and the Skill India campaign aim to address the skill gap and equip the youth with the skills they need to succeed in the 21st-century workforce. However, more needs to be done to ensure that these initiatives reach all sections of society, particularly those from marginalized communities and rural areas.

The pursuit of higher education, while intellectually stimulating, can also be emotionally and mentally taxing for students. The pressure to excel academically, secure internships and jobs, and navigate the complexities of adult life can lead to stress, anxiety, and even depression.

The transition from the structured environment of school to the relative independence of college or university can be challenging for many students. They may experience feelings of loneliness, homesickness, and social isolation,especially if they are away from their families and friends. The pressure to fit in, make new friends, and navigate complex social dynamics can also add to their stress levels.

Moreover, the uncertainty surrounding future career prospects, the fear of failure, and the burden of student loans can weigh heavily on students' minds. The lack of adequate mental health support services on many campuses further exacerbates the problem, leaving students to grapple with their struggles alone.

To address the mental health challenges faced by students, institutions need to create a more supportive and inclusive environment. This includes providing access to mental health professionals, organizing workshops and seminars on stress management and coping skills, and fostering a culture of open communication and support.

Furthermore, it is important to destigmatize mental health issues and encourage students to seek help without fear of judgment or discrimination. Creating awareness about mental health and promoting self-care practices can go a long way in building a more resilient and emotionally healthy student community.

As students embark on the arduous journey through India's education system, they encounter a myriad of challenges that test their resilience, adaptability, and passion for learning. The pressure to excel in a system that often prioritizes rote learning and exams can be overwhelming, leaving students feeling stressed, anxious, and disillusioned. However, amidst these challenges lies the opportunity for transformation and growth. By adopting a proactive and empowered approach, students can navigate this complex landscape and emerge as confident, capable, and fulfilled individuals.

Let us explore strategies and tools that students can utilize to thrive in the Indian education system. and delve into the crucial role of parents in nurturing their children's academic and personal development, providing them with the support and guidance they need to succeed.

To the Students

The Indian education system, with its emphasis on rote learning and exams, can often feel like a daunting and unforgiving terrain. It's messed up, but here we are. Navigation in the system is of great importance and hence, students can equip themselves with a set of tools and strategies to navigate this landscape successfully and emerge as confident, capable, and empowered individuals.

Embrace Self-Directed Learning: Beyond the Classroom Walls

In an era of information overload, the ability to learn independently and critically evaluate information is more important than ever. Don't confine your learning to textbooks and prescribed curricula. Explore a wide range of resources, including online courses, documentaries, books, podcasts, and educational websites. Cultivate a curiosity for knowledge and a passion for lifelong learning. This will not only broaden your horizons but also equip you with the skills and knowledge that employers seek in the 21st century.

Even if you're preparing for a competitive exam, try to focus on what you do over what anyone is asking for you to do. Focus on reading the books you're assigned over staying on a course and set path. Developing that extra edge is of great importance.

Develop Critical Thinking and Problem-Solving Skills

The ability to think critically and solve problems is a valuable asset in any field. Don't just memorize facts; strive to understand the underlying concepts and apply them to real-world situations. Engage in discussions, debates, and projects that challenge you to think creatively and analytically.

Question assumptions, analyze information from multiple perspectives, and evaluate evidence critically. These skills will not only enhance your academic performance but also prepare you for the complexities of the workplace and life in general.

Try to understand the why anything works and how it works. The most dangerous thing in the world is half knowledge. If you know how a motor works, but don't understand it's gist, you will surely mess up.

Seek Mentorship and Guidance

Connect with mentors and role models who can provide guidance, support, and inspiration. This could be teachers,professors, professionals in your field of interest, or even older students who have successfully navigated the system.

Mentors can offer valuable insights, advice, and encouragement, helping you navigate challenges, make informed decisions about your academic and career path, and build a strong professional network.

Prioritize Mental and Physical Health

The pressure of academics can take a toll on your mental and physical health. Make self-care a priority. Get enough sleep, eat healthy, exercise regularly, and engage in activities that bring you joy and relaxation. If you are struggling with stress, anxiety, or depression, don't hesitate to seek help from a counselor or mental health professional. Remember, a healthy mind and body are essential for optimal learning and overall well-being.

Everything can wait, everything can be replaced. You will have endless attempts, but ensure that you're in a good place mentally and physically. No matter what it takes.

Build a Strong Support Network

Surround yourself with positive and supportive people who believe in you and your dreams. This could include family,friends, classmates, or mentors.

A strong support network can provide emotional support, encouragement, and motivation during challenging times. It can also offer a safe space for you to express your concerns, fears, and aspirations without judgment.

Remember, you are not alone in this journey, and seeking help and support is a sign of strength, not weakness.

Embrace Failure as a Learning Opportunity

Don't be afraid to fail. You absolutely will fail. And that's a good thing. Every setback is an opportunity to learn and grow. Develop a growth mindset that embraces challenges and sees failures as stepping stones to success.

Learn from your mistakes, adapt your strategies, and persevere in the face of adversity. Remember, resilience is a key ingredient for success in any endeavor, and the ability to bounce back from setbacks is what separates those who achieve their goals from those who don't.

Find Your Passion and Pursue It

Don't let societal expectations dictate your dreams. Identify your passions and talents, and pursue them with dedication and perseverance. Remember, a fulfilling career is one that aligns with your interests and values. Don't be afraid to explore unconventional paths or take risks.

The journey may be challenging, but the rewards of pursuing your passion are immeasurable. Remember, the world needs individuals who are not afraid to think differently, challenge the status quo, and create their own path.

To the Parents

Parents play a pivotal role in shaping the educational journey of their children. Their support, guidance, and encouragement can make all the difference in a student's success and well-being. Here are some key messages for parents from someone who is in the generation of their wards, on actually developing your child into someone who will be able to function positively in the society:

- **Foster a Love for Learning**: *Beyond the Classroom*

Encourage your children to explore their interests and passions beyond academics. Provide them with opportunities to engage in creative pursuits, sports, and other extracurricular activities that nurture their holistic development. Celebrate their curiosity, encourage them to ask questions, and create a home environment that fosters a love for learning. Remember, learning should be a joyful and enriching experience, not just a means to an end.

- **Set Realistic Expectations:** *The Value of Individuality*

Avoid putting undue pressure on your children to achieve unrealistic academic goals. Recognize and celebrate their unique talents and abilities, and encourage them to pursue their dreams, even if they deviate from the traditional path. Remember, every child is different,and success is not defined solely by academic achievements. Encourage your children to embrace their individuality and pursue their passions, even if they are unconventional or less traveled.

- **Prioritize Mental Health**: *Nurturing Emotional Well-being*

Be mindful of the signs of stress, anxiety, and depression in your children. Create a safe and supportive environment where they feel comfortable sharing their struggles. Seek professional help if needed. Remember, mental health is as important as physical health, and addressing mental health challenges early on can prevent long-term consequences. Encourage open communication, validate their feelings, and provide unconditional love and support.

- **Be a Role Model**: *Leading by Example*

Children learn by observing their parents. Demonstrate a love for learning and a passion for your own work. Your children will learn from your example and be inspired to pursue their own dreams with dedication and perseverance.Show them that learning is a lifelong journey and that success comes in many forms. Be curious, explore new things,and share your experiences with your children. This will not only enrich their lives but also strengthen your bond as a family.

- **Communicate Openly and Honestly**: *Building Trust and Connection*

Maintain open lines of communication with your children. Listen to their concerns, fears, and aspirations without judgment. Offer guidance and support, but also allow them the freedom to make their own choices and learn from their mistakes. Build a relationship based on trust, respect, and mutual understanding. Remember, effective communication is a two-way street, and active listening is as important as expressing your own thoughts and feelings.

- **Celebrate Effort and Progress, Not Just Results**: *Recognizing the Journey*

Focus on your child's effort and progress, not just their grades and ranks. Encourage them to strive for excellence, but also remind them that their worth is not defined by their academic achievements. Celebrate their small victories,acknowledge their struggles, and provide unconditional love and support throughout their journey. Remember, the journey is just as important as the destination, and recognizing their efforts will foster a sense of self-worth and intrinsic motivation.

To the Teachers & Education Institutions

Educators and institutions play a pivotal role in shaping the educational landscape and fostering the holistic development of students. They have the power to create a positive and empowering learning environment that nurtures creativity, critical thinking, and a love for learning.

The curriculum, the backbone of the education system, needs a radical overhaul. The current emphasis on rote learning,memorization, and exam-centric approaches needs to be replaced with a focus on conceptual understanding, critical thinking, problem-solving, and communication skills. The curriculum should be designed to foster curiosity, encourage exploration, and equip students with the skills they need to thrive in the 21st century.

- **Conceptual Understanding:** Move beyond the mere memorization of facts and figures. Encourage students to understand the underlying principles and concepts, enabling them to apply their knowledge in diverse contexts and solve real-world problems. Every teacher I've actually learned from has been very clear on the way they don't teach but help students get to the solution by creating meaningful pathways and mental models.

- **Critical Thinking and Problem-Solving**: Foster a culture of inquiry and exploration. Encourage students to question assumptions, analyze information from multiple perspectives, and evaluate evidence critically. Provide opportunities for them to engage in problem-solving activities, debates, and discussions that challenge their thinking and encourage them to develop their own perspectives. A classroom which is a monologue is the failure of a teacher and the subject will eventually become a problem. If you're a math teacher and your class is a monologue, you're costing the nation future Ramanujans. If you're a biology teacher and your class is a monologue, you just killed a few doctors for the country. If you are a language teacher and are running your class by a monologue, you're affecting the entire workforce as a whole immediately with under qualified individuals who will be constantly underconfident. You're, hence, costing the nation leaders.

- **Communication Skills**: Effective communication is a vital skill in today's interconnected world. The curriculum should incorporate opportunities for students to develop their written and oral communication skills, including presentations, debates, and collaborative projects.

- **Flexibility and Choice:** Offer students more flexibility and choice in their subjects, allowing them to pursue their interests and passions. This will not only enhance their engagement and motivation but also enable them to develop their unique talents and skills. Every student is different and identification of students who do not like the subject matter you cover is of crucial importance as only then can you not push that student to excel and rather focus on the student to take in the bare minimums and work forward.

Technology has the potential to revolutionize the way we teach and learn. Educators and institutions need to embrace technology and leverage its power to create a more engaging, interactive, and personalized learning experience for students.

- **Digital Learning Resources:** Utilize a wide range of digital learning resources, such as online courses,educational videos, simulations, and interactive games, to supplement traditional teaching methods. This can make learning more fun, accessible, and cater to diverse learning styles.

- **Personalized Learning**: Leverage technology to provide personalized learning experiences that cater to the individual needs and abilities of students. Adaptive learning platforms, AI-powered tutoring systems, and data analytics can help track student progress, identify learning gaps, and provide tailored interventions.

- **Collaboration and Communication**: Use technology to foster collaboration and communication among students, teachers, and parents. Online platforms, social media, and communication tools can facilitate discussions, feedback, and sharing of resources, creating a more connected and interactive learning community.

- **Digital Literacy**: Equip students with the digital literacy skills they need to navigate the digital world safely and responsibly. This includes teaching them how to evaluate online information critically, protect their privacy, and use technology ethically and effectively.

The mental health of students is as important as their academic performance. Educators and institutions need to create a safe and supportive environment where students feel comfortable seeking help and talking about their mental health struggles.

Provide access to mental health professionals, such as counselors and psychologists, who can offer counseling and support to students experiencing stress, anxiety, or depression.

Conduct workshops, seminars, and awareness campaigns to destigmatize mental health issues and encourage students to seek help. Train teachers to recognize the signs and symptoms of mental health challenges in their students and provide them with the skills and resources to support their emotional well-being.

Foster a culture of inclusivity and acceptance, where students feel valued and respected regardless of their background, abilities, or challenges.

The relationship between teachers and students can have a profound impact on a student's learning and overall development. Encourage teachers to go beyond their role as instructors and act as mentors and guides, providing personalized support and guidance to each student.

- **Mentorship and Guidance:** Encourage teachers to take a personal interest in their students' academic and personal growth. Provide opportunities for one-on-one interactions, mentoring sessions, and career counseling.
- **Open Communication:** Create a culture of open communication and dialogue where students feel comfortable sharing their thoughts, ideas, and concerns. Encourage teachers to actively listen to their students and provide constructive feedback.
- **Positive Reinforcement**: Recognize and celebrate the efforts and achievements of students, fostering a sense of accomplishment and self-confidence. Provide positive reinforcement and encouragement to motivate students to reach their full potential.

Every student is unique, with their own set of talents, interests, and learning styles. Educators and institutions need to recognize and celebrate this diversity, creating an inclusive environment where every student feels valued and respected.

- **Differentiated Instruction**: Adopt teaching methods that cater to diverse learning styles and abilities. Provide opportunities for students to express themselves creatively and pursue their passions, even if they deviate from the traditional path.
- **Multicultural Education:** Incorporate multicultural perspectives into the curriculum, celebrating the rich cultural heritage of India and promoting understanding and respect for different cultures and traditions.
- **Inclusion and Accessibility:** Ensure that the learning environment is accessible to all students, including those with disabilities. Provide necessary accommodations and support to enable every student to participate fully in the learning process.

Learning should not be confined to the four walls of a classroom. Provide students with opportunities to apply their knowledge in real-world settings through experiential learning activities such as internships, projects, and field trips.This will enable them to develop practical skills, gain valuable insights into different career paths, and make informed choices about their future.

The 21st century demands individuals who can collaborate effectively, think creatively, and innovate solutions to complex problems. Educators and institutions need to foster a culture of collaboration and innovation among students.

- **Teamwork and Collaboration**: Encourage teamwork and collaboration through group projects, discussions, and peer-to-peer learning. This will help students develop essential interpersonal skills, learn from each other, and appreciate the value of diverse perspectives.
- **Creative Problem-Solving**: Provide opportunities for students to engage in creative problem-solving activities that challenge them to think outside the box and come up with innovative solutions.
- **Entrepreneurship and Innovation**: Encourage students to explore their entrepreneurial spirit and develop their ideas into viable businesses or social initiatives. Provide mentorship, resources, and support to help them turn their dreams into reality.

By adopting these strategies and creating a more nurturing and empowering learning environment, educators and institutions can play a crucial role in transforming the Indian education system and preparing students for success in the 21st century. It is a collective responsibility that requires commitment, innovation, and a genuine desire to unleash the full potential of every student.

While the system has undoubtedly produced countless brilliant minds and remarkable achievements, it is also burdened by deeply ingrained systemic issues that hinder the holistic development of its students. The relentless pressure to conform to societal expectations, the exam-centric culture that stifles creativity, the neglect of critical thinking and problem-solving skills, and the persistent inequities in access to quality education all paint a picture of a system in dire need of transformation.

The current state of affairs, while disheartening, is not without hope. Just as the alchemist transforms base metals into gold through dedication, perseverance, and the application of knowledge, so too can we transmute the challenges of our education system into opportunities for growth and progress. It is time to recognize that true education is not merely the accumulation of facts and figures, but the cultivation of a curious, creative, and critical mind. It is about empowering students to become lifelong learners, problem-solvers, and compassionate citizens who can contribute meaningfully to society.

The journey towards a more holistic and empowering education system will undoubtedly be arduous. It will require a concerted effort from all stakeholders - policymakers, educators, parents, students, and society at large. It will demand a willingness to question existing norms, challenge entrenched beliefs, and embrace new ideas and approaches. It will necessitate a shift in mindset, from a narrow focus on academic achievements to a broader vision of education that nurtures the intellectual, emotional, and social development of every child.

Policymakers have a crucial role to play in this transformation. They need to reimagine the curriculum, moving away from rote learning and exam-centric approaches towards a more holistic and skill-based model. The curriculum should be designed to foster curiosity, encourage exploration, and equip students with the skills they need to thrive in the 21st century. It should also be flexible and inclusive, catering to the diverse needs and talents of all students, regardless of their background or abilities.

Educators, the torchbearers of knowledge, need to embrace their role as mentors and guides, fostering a love for learning and empowering students to reach their full potential. They need to adopt innovative teaching methods that encourage critical thinking, creativity, and collaboration. They need to create a safe and supportive learning environment where students feel comfortable expressing themselves, asking questions, and taking risks.

Parents, the first and most influential teachers in a child's life, need to nurture the alchemist's spirit in their children.They need to foster a love for learning, set realistic expectations, and prioritize their children's mental and emotional well-being. They need to encourage their children to explore their passions, even if they deviate from the traditional path, and support them in their journey of self-discovery.

Students, the protagonists of this transformative journey, need to embrace their role as alchemists. They need to be proactive, curious, and resilient, constantly seeking to learn and grow. They need to challenge themselves, step outside their comfort zones, and embrace failure as a learning opportunity. They need to find their voice, express their creativity, and contribute their unique perspectives to the world.

Society at large also has a responsibility to create a conducive environment for educational transformation. We need to challenge stereotypes, celebrate diversity, and value all forms of learning and achievement. We need to create a culture that encourages innovation, risk-taking, and the pursuit of passions.

The challenges facing India's education system are indeed formidable. But they are not insurmountable. By working together, with a shared vision and unwavering commitment, we can transform this system into a catalyst for personal growth, societal progress, and national development. The journey may be long and arduous, but the destination - a brighter and more equitable future for India's youth - is worth striving for. Let us embrace the challenge, nurture the alchemist's spirit in every student, and forge a new era of education that truly empowers and inspires.

Kalam's World

"To become 'developed,' India has to focus on the five areas where India has a core competence for integrated action: (1) Agriculture and food processing; (2) Education and Healthcare; (3) Information and Communication Technology; (4) Infrastructure, reliable and quality electric power, surface transport and infrastructure for all parts of the country; and (5) Self-reliance in critical technologies."

- APJ Abdul Kalam in Vision 2020

Mahabharat

Weeks later, entering into a shady campus with Mohini to express his gratitude, the familiar sight of the ambulance van triggered a cascade of chilling flashbacks as Parth stepped into the hospital courtyard. The metallic clang of its doors, the haunting wail of its siren - they transported him back to that fateful night, the blur of flashing lights and the suffocating darkness. His hand instinctively reached for Mohini's, seeking solace in her presence as they navigated the bustling corridors.

The general ward, once a scene of his own suffering, now evoked a different kind of unease. The overcrowded beds, the chorus of moans and coughs, the harried nurses - it was a stark reminder of the fragility of life and the relentless challenges faced by those less fortunate. A wave of gratitude washed over him, tempered by a profound sense of survivor's guilt.

They found Dr. Nakul in the doctor's lounge, a steaming cup of tea in his hand, engaged in a lively conversation with Dr. Nandini. Nakul's face lit up upon seeing Parth. "Parth? It's so good to see you back on your feet!" He turned to Nandini, his voice brimming with admiration. "This is the young man I was telling you about, the one Dr. Madhav saved the day when the bus toppled from the bridge. I saved him… along with sir."

Nandini smiled warmly, her eyes filled with compassion. "Dr. Madhav is on his break right now. First floor, third room."

Parth's cheeks flushed with a mix of embarrassment and gratitude. He followed Nakul down a dimly lit corridor, the walls adorned with peeling paint and faded posters. They reached a small, unassuming room, its door slightly ajar. Nakul knocked gently, then pushed it open.

Dr. Madhav sat at a cluttered desk, a plate of rajma chawal balanced precariously amidst a sea of medical journals and patient files. He looked up, his face breaking into a wide smile. "Come in, come in!"

Parth and Mohini entered the cramped space, a stark contrast to the gleaming offices Madhav must have occupied in the US. The air hung heavy with the scent of spices and old paper, a strangely comforting aroma that spoke of dedication and long hours.

"Thank you sir" Parth began, his voice thick with emotion. "For everything. You saved my life."

Madhav waved a dismissive hand. "It was my duty, Parth. And you're a strong young man. You fought hard."

As they settled into the mismatched chairs, Parth's gaze fell upon a framed quote on the wall:

"The meaning of life is to find your gift. The purpose of life is to give it away." - William Shakespeare

He turned to Madhav, his heart filled with a thousand questions. "Sir, how did you know what to do? How did you make the right decisions, even with so little?"

Madhav chuckled, a twinkle in his eye. "Parth, life is a constant battle and we are the privileged. We are all warriors, fighting our own battles, facing our own challenges. But the key is to focus on the present, on the task at hand. Performing your own duties."

He paused, his gaze thoughtful. "I have endless patients coming in, and just like any doctor, I just perform my duties without attachment to the outcome. It's crucial to ensure you're calm and composed for your patient's life. The results of our actions are not in our control, so we should not let them define us. Especially in my profession. Our focus should be on doing our best, with complete dedication and sincerity. And that's all I do."

Parth nodded, his mind absorbing Madhav's words. "But sir," he hesitated, "why did you come back to India? You could have had a successful career in the US."

Madhav's smile widened. "India is my country, Parth. I'll not say the cliche, 'It's where my heart belongs.' But there are endless opportunities here to make a real difference, to serve those who need it most. I became a doctor to save lives. And these are the lives which give my mission a meaning."

He leaned forward, his eyes sparkling with passion. "This country is brimming with potential, Parth. It's a land of challenges, yes, but also of immense possibilities. And it's up to us, the youth, to seize those opportunities, to fight for a better future, not just for ourselves, but for generations to come."

Parth's heart swelled with a newfound sense of purpose. Madhav's words had ignited a spark within him, a desire to rise above his past failures and contribute to something greater than himself. As he left the hospital, the weight of his burdens seemed lighter, replaced by a glimmer of hope for the future.

He knew what he had to do now…

India, a land of vibrant colors, ancient traditions, and rapid modernization, presents a fascinating paradox. Its rich tapestry is woven with threads of a glorious past intertwined with the aspirations of a rapidly developing nation. The country is a melting pot of diverse cultures, languages, and religions, creating a unique mosaic of human experience.Amidst this dynamic landscape lies a nation teeming with immense potential and formidable challenges. India's journey is a testament to its resilience and determination to carve a path toward progress and prosperity. This chapter embarks on an exploration of the multifaceted reality of India, delving into its opportunities and challenges across various sectors and societal aspects.

India's youthful population, with over 65% of its people under the age of 35, represents a significant asset, often referred to as the "demographic dividend." This burgeoning young workforce has the potential to fuel India's economic growth and propel it to new heights. However, realizing this potential necessitates strategic investments in education,skill development, and employment opportunities.

Quality education and skill development are paramount in harnessing the potential of India's youth. The government's initiatives like the "Skill India" mission aim to equip young people with the skills required for the 21st-century workforce. However, challenges persist in ensuring access to quality education, particularly in rural areas, and bridging the gap between theoretical knowledge and practical skills. The private sector, educational institutions, and non-governmental organizations must collaborate to create a robust ecosystem that fosters skill development and empowers young people to pursue their dreams.

India's youth are increasingly embracing entrepreneurship and innovation, driven by a desire to create solutions and contribute to society. The startup ecosystem in India is thriving, with young entrepreneurs disrupting traditional industries and creating new avenues for growth. From technology and healthcare to agriculture and renewable energy,young Indians are making a mark globally with their innovative ideas and ventures.

Despite the immense potential, India's youth face numerous challenges. Unemployment and underemployment remain significant concerns, exacerbated by the COVID-19 pandemic. Lack of access to quality education, especially in rural areas, limits opportunities for many young people. Social inequalities, including gender disparities and discrimination based on caste and religion, further hinder their progress.

The government, private sector, and civil society are actively working to address the challenges faced by India's youth. Initiatives like the "Startup India" program provide support and incentives to young entrepreneurs. We ourselves received our first fund from the Startup India Seed Fund Scheme.

Skill development programs, apprenticeships, and vocational training are being promoted to enhance employability. Educational reforms are underway to improve the quality of education and make it more relevant to the needs of the job market. By empowering its youth and creating opportunities for them to thrive, India can unlock its true potential and achieve sustainable development.

The disparity in healthcare access and infrastructure between rural and urban areas is a major concern. While urban centers boast modern hospitals and specialized medical facilities, rural communities often lack basic healthcare infrastructure and qualified healthcare professionals. This divide results in unequal access to healthcare services and perpetuates health inequities.

India grapples with a complex disease burden, including communicable diseases like tuberculosis and malaria, non-communicable diseases like diabetes and heart disease, maternal and child health issues, and mental health concerns.Addressing this multifaceted challenge requires a comprehensive approach that focuses on prevention, early detection,treatment, and rehabilitation.

The government has launched several initiatives to improve healthcare access and affordability. The Ayushman Bharat scheme, touted as the world's largest health insurance program, aims to provide health coverage to millions of poor and vulnerable families. The private sector plays a crucial role in supplementing government efforts, with private hospitals and clinics providing a significant portion of healthcare services.

Achieving universal healthcare coverage and improving overall health and well-being in India necessitates a multi-pronged approach. Strengthening primary healthcare infrastructure, especially in rural areas, is essential. Investing in preventive healthcare programs, promoting health awareness, and addressing social determinants of health are crucial.Leveraging technology and innovation can improve healthcare delivery and make it more accessible and affordable.Public-private partnerships can further enhance the reach and effectiveness of healthcare services.

India's commitment to providing free and compulsory education to all children is enshrined in its Constitution. The Right to Education Act, enacted in 2009, aims to ensure that every child between the ages of 6 and 14 receives quality education. While significant progress has been made in increasing enrollment rates, challenges persist in ensuring quality education and bridging the learning gap.

The focus on increasing enrollment rates has sometimes come at the expense of quality education. Teacher training,infrastructure development, and curriculum reform are crucial to improve the quality of education. Addressing the shortage of qualified teachers, particularly in rural areas, is imperative. Providing adequate infrastructure, including classrooms, libraries, and laboratories, is essential for creating a conducive learning environment. The curriculum needs to be updated regularly to keep pace with the changing needs of the job market and equip students with the skills required for the 21st century.

A significant challenge facing India's education system is the mismatch between the skills imparted and the demands of the job market. Many graduates lack the practical skills and industry-relevant knowledge required for employment.Bridging this skill gap necessitates closer collaboration between educational institutions and industries. Vocational training, apprenticeships, and internship programs can help students gain practical experience and enhance their employability.

The digital divide, particularly in rural areas, poses a significant challenge to equitable access to education. The COVID-19 pandemic highlighted the importance of technology-enabled learning, but lack of access to devices and internet connectivity limited opportunities for many students. Bridging the digital divide requires investment in infrastructure, providing affordable devices, and promoting digital literacy.

Technology has the potential to transform education in India. E-learning platforms, online courses, and skill development platforms can provide access to quality education and training to students in remote areas and those who cannot attend traditional educational institutions. Technology can also personalize learning, making it more engaging and effective. By embracing technology and integrating it into the education system, India can enhance learning outcomes and equip its youth with the skills required for the future.

India's economic growth trajectory has been impressive, with the country emerging as one of the fastest-growing major economies in the world. Its vast market, young workforce, and increasing urbanization offer significant opportunities for growth and development. India's potential as a global economic powerhouse is undeniable, but realizing this potential requires addressing various challenges and harnessing opportunities in key sectors.

Several factors can potentially hinder India's economic progress. Infrastructure bottlenecks, including inadequate transportation networks and power supply, can impede productivity and increase costs. Bureaucratic hurdles and regulatory complexities can discourage investment and hinder business growth. Income inequality, with a significant portion of the population living in poverty, can limit domestic demand and create social unrest. Addressing these challenges requires concerted efforts from the government, private sector, and civil society.

There are various fields and sectors in today's time which are constantly booming:

India's IT sector is a global leader, known for its skilled workforce and innovative solutions. The sector has created millions of jobs and contributed significantly to India's economic growth. Technology also plays a crucial role in improving healthcare delivery, transforming education, and enhancing efficiency across various sectors.

The "Make in India" initiative aims to boost manufacturing and transform India into a global manufacturing hub. This sector has the potential to create millions of jobs and drive economic growth. However, it requires investment in infrastructure, skill development, and technology adoption.

Agriculture remains the backbone of India's economy, providing livelihoods to a large portion of the population. However, the sector faces challenges like climate change, farmer distress, and low productivity. Sustainable practices, technology adoption, and agribusiness development can enhance agricultural productivity and improve farmers' incomes.

India is committed to transitioning to a clean energy future. The renewable energy sector offers immense opportunities for job creation, reduced emissions, and sustainable development. Investments in solar, wind, and other renewable energy sources are crucial for achieving India's energy goals.

Our rich cultural heritage, diverse landscapes, and natural beauty attract millions of tourists every year. The tourism and hospitality sector has significant potential for job creation and revenue generation. However, it requires investment in infrastructure, skill development, and marketing.

The government's focus on infrastructure development, including roads, railways,ports, and airports, is crucial for improving connectivity and boosting economic growth. This sector offers opportunities for youth in engineering, construction, and other related fields.

These are all opportunities. Opportunities for development, and for investment. And with increasing private investment in public domains, there's huge scope for development.

The government plays a crucial role in creating a conducive environment for economic growth and development. Policies and initiatives that promote investment, ease of doing business, and skill development are essential.

The private sector is a key driver of economic growth, creating jobs and contributing to innovation. Collaboration between the government and the private sector is crucial for achieving sustainable and inclusive development.

India's economic growth must be inclusive and sustainable, benefiting all segments of society and protecting the environment. Ensuring equitable access to opportunities, reducing poverty, and addressing social inequalities are essential for achieving sustainable development. Investing in renewable energy, promoting sustainable agriculture, and adopting green technologies are crucial for protecting the environment and mitigating the impact of climate change.

India's rich cultural diversity is a source of strength and pride. The country is home to people of various religions,languages, and ethnicities, creating a vibrant tapestry of human experience. Fostering an inclusive society where everyone feels valued and respected, regardless of their background, is crucial for social progress and harmony.

At the same time, achieving gender equality remains a significant challenge in India. Women face discrimination and inequality in various aspects of life, including education, employment, and decision-making. However, progress has been made in recent years, with increased female literacy rates, greater participation in the workforce, and initiatives to empower women economically and socially. Continued efforts are needed to address deep-rooted gender biases and create a more equitable society.

The nation as a whole can only sustain if the women in the country are given proper rights and as much as we try to justify equal opportunities for women in urban areas, a lot of work is yet to be done in areas. Even in urban areas, there are various women who are underrepresented and undergo regular abuse and violence silently. Mental torture and years of conditioning have still silenced various household fires. And to top it all off, the rapidly increasing number of rapes in the corners of the country have escalated to the centers now.

The invisible work of various sects is another crucial issue for the country. Be it women, be it the working class or be it the blue collar executives.

Social inequalities based on caste, religion, and other factors persist in India, hindering social progress and inclusion.The government and civil society organizations are working to address these inequalities through affirmative action programs, awareness campaigns, and legal reforms. Promoting social justice and ensuring equal opportunities for all,regardless of their background, is crucial for building a harmonious and prosperous society.

Marginalized communities, including Scheduled Castes, Scheduled Tribes, and other backward classes, face numerous challenges in accessing education, healthcare, and economic opportunities. Initiatives aimed at empowering these communities, including reservations in education and employment, skill development programs, and financial assistance, are crucial for ensuring their participation in India's development.

Civil society organizations play a crucial role in promoting social progress and inclusion in India. They work tirelessly to raise awareness about social issues, advocate for policy changes, and implement programs that empower marginalized communities. Their efforts complement government initiatives and contribute significantly to building a more equitable and just society.

India's journey is a testament to its resilience, determination, and unwavering spirit. The country's youthful population, rich cultural heritage, and economic potential offer immense opportunities for growth and development. However, challenges such as poverty, inequality, and environmental degradation persist. Addressing these challenges and harnessing the opportunities effectively requires a concerted effort from the government, private sector, and civil society.

Investing in education, skill development, and healthcare is crucial for empowering India's youth and creating a healthy and productive workforce. Promoting entrepreneurship and innovation can unleash the creative potential of young people and drive economic growth. Bridging the digital divide and ensuring equitable access to technology-enabled learning can transform education and create opportunities for all.

India's economic growth must be inclusive and sustainable, benefiting all segments of society and protecting the environment. Policies and initiatives that promote investment, ease of doing business, and skill development are essential. Collaboration between the government and the private sector is crucial for achieving sustainable and inclusive development.

Fostering an inclusive society where everyone feels valued and respected, regardless of their background, is crucial for social progress and harmony. Achieving gender equality, addressing social inequalities, and empowering marginalized communities require continued efforts from all stakeholders.

India's future is bright, but realizing its full potential requires addressing its challenges and harnessing its opportunities effectively. The road ahead may be long and arduous, but with determination, innovation, and collaboration, India can achieve its aspirations and create a better future for all its citizens.

Each one of us has a role to play in shaping India's future. Whether it's through education, entrepreneurship, social activism, or simply being a responsible citizen, we can all contribute to India's growth and development. Let us embrace the opportunities and challenges that lie ahead with optimism and determination, working together to build a stronger, more inclusive, and prosperous India.

Ramayan

The weeks following Parth's return home were a whirlwind of introspection and exploration. The confines of his room, once a sanctuary of comfort, now transformed into a laboratory of ideas. He spent countless hours poring over books, browsing the internet, and engaging in deep conversations with Mohini and his parents. His mind, once clouded by despair, was now ablaze with a newfound curiosity and a burning desire to make a difference.

One afternoon, as he sat on his balcony, watching the vibrant tapestry of life unfold in the streets below, a thought struck him. The local market, a bustling hub of activity, was overflowing with plastic waste. Vendors used plastic bags indiscriminately, and customers discarded them without a second thought, contributing to the growing environmental crisis.

Parth's mind raced. He remembered a documentary he had watched about the harmful effects of plastic on marine life and ecosystems. He thought about the overflowing landfills, the polluted waterways, and the countless animals suffering from plastic ingestion.

An idea began to take shape. What if there was a way to handle and clear out all this waste? Something biodegradable, eco-friendly, and readily available? He shared his thoughts with Mohini, who was immediately enthusiastic.

"That's an interesting idea!" she exclaimed. "We can look for ways to eliminate plastic waste somehow."

Parth's eyes lit up. "Waste elimination is the most important thing in the current market. How do we eliminate all this that we've created."

The idea grew, fueled by their shared passion for the environment and their desire to make a tangible impact. They spent hours researching different materials, designing prototypes, and exploring potential funding options. They faced challenges, of course. Some people dismissed their idea as idealistic, while others questioned their ability to compete with the established companies.

But Parth and Mohini refused to be discouraged. They drew strength from their shared vision and their determination to create a better future. They organised awareness campaigns in their college, educating their peers about the harmful effects of plastic and the importance of sustainable alternatives, building a team of motivated people. They reached out to local NGOs and environmental groups, seeking guidance and support in the form of funds to work on the project.

As their project gained momentum, Parth felt a sense of purpose he had never experienced before. He was no longer a passive observer, but an active participant in shaping his world. The challenges he faced, the setbacks he encountered,only fueled his resolve. He was learning, growing, and making a difference, one thing at a time.

The journey was just beginning, but Parth knew that he was on the right path.

The epic Ramayana, a cornerstone of Indian culture and heritage, narrates a tale of governance, leadership, and the triumph of good over evil. Central to the narrative is the concept of 'Rama Rajya,' an idealized state of governance marked by decentralization, righteousness, and prosperity for all. As India navigates the complexities of the 21st century, there is a growing resonance with the principles of Rama Rajya, particularly the shift from centralization to decentralization.

For much of its post-independence history, India followed a centralized model of governance, with power concentrated in the hands of the central government. While this approach had its merits, particularly in nation-building and maintaining unity in a diverse country, it also led to inefficiencies, bureaucratic hurdles, and a disconnect between policymakers and the people they served.

The winds of change, however, are blowing across the Indian landscape. There's a palpable shift towards decentralization, a move that echoes the essence of the future. The 73rd and 74th Constitutional Amendments, passed in 1992, marked a watershed moment in this journey. These amendments empowered local self-governments - Panchayati Raj Institutions (PRIs) in rural areas and Urban Local Bodies (ULBs) in urban areas - giving them a greater say in decision-making and resource allocation.

This decentralization has the potential to transform India in profound ways. By bringing governance closer to the people, it can lead to more responsive and accountable administration. Local leaders, deeply rooted in their communities, are better equipped to understand the needs and aspirations of their constituents. This can result in more effective and targeted policies, leading to improved service delivery in areas such as education, healthcare, sanitation,and infrastructure development.

Moreover, decentralization can foster a sense of ownership and participation among citizens. When people have a say in how their communities are governed and how resources are utilized, they are more likely to be invested in the development process. This can unleash a wave of civic engagement and grassroots innovation, leading to more sustainable and inclusive growth.

The rise of local leadership, particularly among women, is a particularly heartening aspect of this decentralization drive. The reservation of seats for women in PRIs and ULBs has opened doors for their participation in the political process. Women leaders, often more attuned to the needs of marginalized groups, are bringing a fresh perspective to governance, championing issues such as education for girls, maternal and child health, and women's economic empowerment.

The scenario of women in India is a complex web with threads of progress and persistent challenges. While the constitutional amendments have paved the way for greater political participation, women continue to face deeply ingrained social and cultural barriers.

Patriarchy, gender stereotypes, and limited access to education and economic opportunities hinder their full potential.

However, the winds of change are blowing. A growing number of women are breaking the glass ceiling, excelling in various fields, and challenging traditional norms. From politics and business to science and the arts, women are making their mark and inspiring others to follow suit. The reservation of seats in local bodies has been instrumental in this transformation, providing a platform for women to showcase their leadership skills and advocate for change.

Yet, much work remains to be done. Addressing the root causes of gender inequality requires a multi-pronged approach.Investing in education for girls, promoting women's economic empowerment, and challenging discriminatory social norms are crucial steps. It also necessitates creating a safe and enabling environment where women can thrive without fear of violence or harassment.

The journey towards gender equality is a long and arduous one, but it is a journey that India must undertake.Empowering women is not just a moral imperative; it is also a key driver of economic growth and social progress. A society that values and respects its women is a society that is more just, equitable, and prosperous for all.

Alongside the decentralization of governance, India is also witnessing a transformation in its economic landscape. The liberalization of the economy in the early 1990s marked a turning point, opening doors for private sector participation and market-driven growth. Privatization, the transfer of ownership and control of state-owned enterprises to private entities, has been a key component of this economic reform agenda.

The impact of privatization has been a subject of intense debate. Proponents argue that it leads to greater efficiency,improved service delivery, and increased investment in infrastructure and technology. Private companies, driven by profit motives, are incentivized to innovate, optimize operations, and cater to consumer demands. This can lead to better quality products and services, lower prices, and greater choice for consumers.

However, critics raise concerns about the potential downsides of privatization. They argue that it can lead to job losses,widening income disparities, and reduced access to essential services for marginalized groups. Private companies,driven by profit maximization, may prioritize commercially viable areas, neglecting unprofitable but socially important sectors such as healthcare and education in rural areas.

Furthermore, the lack of adequate regulatory oversight can lead to monopolistic practices, price gouging, and exploitation of consumers. The privatization of natural resources and essential services, such as water and electricity,can also raise concerns about affordability and accessibility for the poor.

The market-driven economy, while unleashing entrepreneurial energies and driving economic growth, has also created new challenges. The increasing emphasis on competition and efficiency has led to a growing sense of insecurity and uncertainty among workers. The rise of automation and technological advancements is further disrupting traditional job markets, raising concerns about job displacement and the need for reskilling and upskilling.

In this context, the emergence of the gig economy is a significant development. Characterized by short-term contracts, freelance work, and platform-based employment, the gig economy is transforming the nature of work and employment relationships. For many young people, the gig economy offers flexibility, autonomy, and the opportunity to pursue their passions. It also provides a platform for those with specialized skills and expertise to connect with clients and employers across the globe.

The gig economy has the potential to empower youth and drive job creation, particularly in sectors such as technology, creative arts, and online services. It can also provide opportunities for women and those in rural areas to participate in the workforce and earn a livelihood.

However, the gig economy also comes with its share of challenges. The lack of social security benefits, job insecurity, and the potential for exploitation are major concerns.

Moreover, the gig economy often lacks the traditional structures of employment, such as unions and collective bargaining, making it difficult for workers to negotiate fair wages and working conditions. It is essential to create a regulatory framework that balances the flexibility and dynamism of the gig economy with the need to protect workers' rights and ensure decent work for all.

In the midst of these economic transformations, entrepreneurship is emerging as a key driver of India's growth story. A new generation of entrepreneurs, armed with innovative ideas and a passion for problem-solving, is disrupting traditional industries and creating new markets. From e-commerce and fintech to healthcare and education, startups are challenging the status quo and driving innovation across sectors.

The success stories of Indian startups are inspiring. Companies like Flipkart, Paytm, Ola, and Byju's have not only created enormous wealth but also transformed the way Indians shop, pay, travel, and learn. These companies have leveraged technology to reach millions of customers, providing access to products and services that were previously unavailable or unaffordable.

Moreover, these startups have created thousands of jobs, particularly for young people. They have also fostered a culture of innovation and risk-taking, inspiring others to pursue their entrepreneurial dreams. The government's initiatives, such as the Startup India program, have further fueled this entrepreneurial spirit, providing support and incentives for startups to thrive.

The impact of entrepreneurship goes beyond economic growth. It also has a profound social impact. Startups are addressing some of India's most pressing challenges, from providing affordable healthcare and clean energy to improving access to education and financial services for the underserved. They are also creating a more inclusive and equitable society, providing opportunities for people from all walks of life to participate in the economic mainstream.

The journey towards a decentralized, entrepreneurial India is not without its challenges. It requires a reimagining of governance, a rethinking of economic policies, and a reorientation of social attitudes. It also necessitates addressing deep-rooted inequalities and ensuring that the benefits of growth are shared by all.

However, the potential rewards are immense. A decentralized India, where governance is more responsive and opportunities are more accessible, can unleash the creative energies of its people and create a more just and prosperous society. An entrepreneurial India, where innovation and risk-taking are celebrated, can drive economic growth and create jobs for millions.

The vision of Rama Rajya, or a utopian, decentralized state where righteousness and prosperity prevail, may seem like a distant dream. But it is a dream that India can strive towards. By embracing the principles of decentralization, empowering its people, and fostering a culture of entrepreneurship, India can create a future that is both inclusive and prosperous.

The journey may be long and arduous, but the destination is worth striving for. A decentralized, entrepreneurial India is not just a vision; it is a possibility within reach. It is a testament to the enduring power of the Ramayana's ideals and a beacon of hope for a nation on the cusp of transformation.

As India stands at this critical juncture, it is imperative to embrace the spirit of sustainable development and forge a path towards a more decentralized and entrepreneurial future. This entails empowering local communities, fostering a culture of innovation, and creating an enabling environment for businesses to thrive. It also necessitates addressing the challenges of inequality, ensuring that the benefits of growth are shared by all, and creating a society that is both just and prosperous.

The journey towards a decentralized, entrepreneurial India requires a multi-faceted approach. It begins with strengthening local governance institutions, providing them with adequate resources and autonomy to make decisions that are in the best interests of their communities. It also involves investing in education and skill development,empowering individuals with the knowledge and capabilities to participate in the modern economy.

Furthermore, it necessitates creating a level playing field for businesses, reducing bureaucratic hurdles, and promoting fair competition. This includes simplifying regulations, streamlining licensing procedures, and providing access to finance for entrepreneurs, particularly those from marginalized communities. It also entails fostering a culture of innovation, encouraging risk-taking, and celebrating entrepreneurial success.

The role of technology in this transformation cannot be overstated. Digital technologies have the potential to revolutionize governance, making it more transparent, efficient, and accessible. They can also empower citizens,providing them with information and tools to participate in the decision-making process. Furthermore, technology can facilitate the growth of the gig economy, connecting individuals with opportunities across the globe and enabling them to earn a livelihood.

However, the digital divide remains a significant challenge. Access to technology and digital literacy are not evenly distributed, particularly in rural areas and among marginalized communities. Bridging this divide is essential to ensure that the benefits of technology are shared by all and that no one is left behind in the digital age.

The journey towards a decentralized, entrepreneurial India is not just about economic growth and technological advancements. It is also about creating a society that is more equitable, inclusive, and sustainable. This entails addressing the root causes of inequality, such as poverty, discrimination, and lack of access to basic services. It also involves promoting environmental sustainability, ensuring that economic growth does not come at the cost of the planet.

The vision of Rama Rajya, a decentralized state where righteousness and prosperity prevail, is a powerful reminder of India's rich cultural heritage and its enduring values. It is a vision that can inspire and guide India as it navigates the complexities of the 21st century. By embracing the principles of decentralization, empowering its people, and fostering a culture of entrepreneurship, India can create a future that is both inclusive and prosperous.

The challenges are many, but the opportunities are even greater. India stands at the cusp of a new era, an era where the spirit of Rama Rajya can guide its journey towards a more decentralized, entrepreneurial, and equitable future. It is a journey that requires courage, determination, and a unwavering commitment to the ideals of justice, equality, and prosperity for all.

This journey towards a decentralized and entrepreneurial India is not merely a theoretical construct; it is a dynamic process that is already reshaping the socio-economic landscape of the country. In the heartland of rural India,Panchayati Raj Institutions are not just administrative bodies; they are catalysts for grassroots empowerment. They are enabling villagers to participate in decision-making processes that directly impact their lives, from the allocation of funds for infrastructure projects to the implementation of welfare schemes. This bottom-up approach to governance is fostering a sense of ownership and responsibility among citizens, leading to more sustainable and inclusive development.

In the bustling metropolises, the winds of change are equally palpable. Urban Local Bodies are increasingly adopting participatory planning models, involving residents in the design and execution of urban development projects. This is not only leading to more livable and vibrant cities but also fostering a sense of belonging and civic pride among urban dwellers. The smart city initiatives, with their focus on technology-driven solutions and citizen engagement, are further accelerating this transformation.

The government's role in this transformation is crucial. It is not just about creating an enabling environment for businesses; it is also about investing in human capital, promoting digital literacy, and fostering a culture of innovation.The initiatives such as the Startup India program, Digital India campaign, and Skill India mission are all steps in the right direction. However, more needs to be done to bridge the digital divide, address the skill gap, and create a level playing field for all entrepreneurs.

The journey towards a decentralized, entrepreneurial India is not without its complexities. The challenges of inequality,social prejudices, and bureaucratic hurdles persist. The rapid pace of technological change and globalization is creating new uncertainties and anxieties. The fear of job displacement, the erosion of traditional social structures, and the widening gap between the rich and the poor are all legitimate concerns that need to be addressed.

Yet, amidst these challenges, there is also a sense of optimism and hope. The spirit of entrepreneurship, the power of technology, and the growing aspirations of the people are all driving forces for change. India stands at a crossroads,with the potential to create a future that is both inclusive and prosperous.

The vision of a decentralized, entrepreneurial India is not just a dream; it is an imperative. It is a vision that can harness the creative energies of its people, unleash the power of innovation, and create a society that is both just and prosperous. It is a vision that can inspire India to achieve its full potential and become a beacon of hope for the world.

The journey may be long and arduous, but the destination is worth striving for. A decentralized, entrepreneurial India is not just a possibility; it is a destiny waiting to be fulfilled. It is a testament to the enduring spirit of the Indian people and their unwavering commitment to the ideals of a society where righteousness, prosperity, and happiness prevail for all.

The Road Ahead

"We always overestimate the change that will occur in the next two years and underestimate the change that will occur in the next ten. Don't let yourself be lulled into inaction."

- Bill Gates in The Road Ahead

Metamorphosis

The sleek auditorium at IIT Delhi buzzed with anticipation. It was their E-Summit, and a panel of distinguished alumni had gathered to inspire the next generation of innovators. Parth, his once-bandaged face now bearing only faint scars, stood at the podium, his presence radiating confidence and success. A huge banner of Parth's $16B company, Karma, stood on the backdrop.

He had come a long way since his accident, transforming his pain into purpose and building a thriving social enterprise focused on sustainable solutions. The company crossed various rounds and as money started pouring in, Parth even got his hands deeply involved in Philanthropy. His journey had been fraught with challenges, but he had persevered, driven by his unwavering belief in his vision and his commitment to making a positive impact.

As he addressed the eager audience, Parth's gaze swept across the sea of faces, his own experiences mirroring the aspirations and anxieties reflected in their eyes.

Someone in the audience stood up with a mic, "How do you stay motivated and so well composed in times when there's absolute panic everywhere. Especially in the recent market situations where every company's stake only fell while Karma pushed through."

"When I was sitting where you are now," he began, his voice warm and engaging, "I was plagued by doubts and uncertainties. I had no idea what I wanted to do with my life, let alone how to achieve it."

He paused, allowing his words to sink in. "But then, a series of events, both tragic and transformative, led me to discover my purpose. I realized that the true measure of success lies not in accolades or material wealth, but in the efforts you put in to bring impact towards the world around us."

A hush fell over the room as Parth shared his story, his words painting a vivid picture of his journey from despair to empowerment. He spoke of his accident, his struggles with self-doubt, and the unwavering support of his family and mentors. He spoke of his passion for sustainability and his determination to create a business that not only generated profits but also contributed to a better future.

"One of the most important lessons I learned," Parth continued, his voice resonating with conviction, "is to focus on the present, on the task at hand. Just as Arjuna in the Bhagavad Gita was guided by Krishna to fulfil his dharma without attachment to the outcome, I too strive to act with integrity, dedication, and a genuine desire to make a positive impact."

He paused, his gaze meeting the eyes of a young woman in the front row, her expression mirroring his own past anxieties.

"Don't be afraid to dream big," he encouraged her, his voice filled with warmth. "Don't let fear or self-doubt hold you back. Find your purpose, your Kurukshetra, and pursue it with unwavering passion. The path may not always be clear, but as long as you act with sincerity and a commitment to making a difference, you will find your way."

In the grand theater of nature, the butterfly's metamorphosis stands as a testament to the transformative power of change. It begins its existence as a humble caterpillar, earthbound and constrained, its potential seemingly limited by its form. Yet, through a remarkable and awe-inspiring process of metamorphosis, it sheds its former self, emerging from its chrysalis as a breathtaking creature with vibrant wings, capable of soaring to unimaginable heights, transcending its previous limitations and embracing a world of possibilities.

India, much like the caterpillar, stands at a pivotal juncture in its history. To unleash its boundless potential and ascend to its rightful place among the world's leading nations, it must embark on a journey of metamorphosis, shedding its outdated paradigms and embracing a new identity. This transformation is not merely a superficial makeover, a change of clothes or a fresh coat of paint. It is a profound and holistic shift, a metamorphosis that reaches into the very core of our being, altering the way we think, act, and engage with the world around us. It is a transformation that will touch every aspect of our society, from the individual to the collective, from the economic to the social, from the political to the cultural.

This metamorphosis is not a choice, but an imperative. The world is changing at an unprecedented pace, driven by technological advancements, globalization, and shifting geopolitical realities. To thrive in this new world, India must adapt and evolve. It must shed its old skin, its outdated beliefs and practices, and emerge as a vibrant, dynamic, and forward-looking nation. It must embrace change not as a threat, but as an opportunity, a chance to reinvent itself and create a better future for all its citizens.

The journey of transformation will not be easy. It will require courage, determination, and a willingness to challenge the status quo. It will demand sacrifices and compromises, as we navigate the complexities of change and grapple with the inevitable growing pains. But the rewards of this journey are immense. A transformed India will be a nation that is strong, prosperous, and just. It will be a nation that is a leader in the 21st century and beyond, a beacon of hope and progress for the world.

Change, even when it heralds a brighter future, often encounters resistance. This resistance is not merely a matter of stubbornness or inertia; it is deeply ingrained in our psychology, both at the individual and societal levels. It arises from a primal fear of the unknown, a reluctance to venture beyond the familiar confines of our comfort zones, and a yearning to cling to the known, even when it no longer serves our best interests.

At the individual level, people resist change because it disrupts their sense of security and control. The familiar, even if it is flawed or limiting, offers a sense of predictability and comfort. Change, on the other hand, introduces uncertainty and the possibility of failure. It challenges our assumptions and beliefs, forcing us to confront our limitations and step outside the boundaries of our comfort zones. This can be a daunting prospect, triggering a natural instinct to resist.

Moreover, change often involves loss. It may mean letting go of old habits, relationships, or ways of life. It may require us to acquire new skills or adapt to new technologies. These losses, even if they pave the way for future gains, can be painful and difficult to accept. This fear of loss, coupled with the uncertainty of the future, can create a powerful resistance to change at the individual level.

At the societal level, resistance to change is often fueled by entrenched power structures and vested interests. Those who derive benefits from the current system, whether they are political leaders, business tycoons, or social elites, are naturally averse to any alteration that might threaten their position or privileges. They wield their influence to preserve the status quo, erecting barriers to progress and stifling innovation. They may use propaganda, misinformation, or even coercion to maintain their grip on power and prevent any meaningful change from taking place.

Furthermore, societal resistance to change can also stem from deeply ingrained cultural norms and traditions. Societies,like individuals, often develop a sense of identity and belonging based on their shared history, values, and practices.Change, especially if it is perceived as a threat to these core elements of identity, can trigger a backlash. This is particularly true in societies with strong traditional or religious values, where change may be seen as an attack on the very fabric of society.

Overcoming this resistance, both at the individual and societal levels, is a complex and multifaceted challenge. It requires a multi-pronged approach that addresses the psychological, social, and structural barriers to change.

At the individual level, it involves fostering a mindset of openness and adaptability. It means encouraging people to embrace change as an opportunity for growth and development, rather than a threat to their security. It requires providing them with the tools and resources they need to navigate the complexities of change, such as education,training, and support networks.

At the societal level, it involves challenging entrenched power structures and vested interests. It means creating a more inclusive and participatory decision-making process, where the voices of all stakeholders are heard and considered. It requires promoting transparency and accountability, so that those in power are held responsible for their actions and decisions.

Moreover, overcoming resistance to change requires effective communication and leadership. It is essential to articulate a clear and compelling vision for the future, one that inspires hope and motivates people to embrace change. It is equally important to address people's fears and concerns, to provide them with reassurance and support, and to demonstrate that change can be a positive and empowering force.

Transformation is not a seamless journey, devoid of challenges or setbacks. Like the caterpillar undergoing metamorphosis, India will inevitably experience growing pains as it sheds its old skin and emerges into a new reality.There will be obstacles and setbacks, moments of doubt and uncertainty, as the nation grapples with the complexities of change and adapts to new ways of being. But these discomforts are not a sign of failure or weakness; they are an integral part of the journey, a testament to the profound changes taking place within the nation's fabric.

Change, by its very nature, disrupts the established order. It compels us to confront our limitations, to question our assumptions, and to venture beyond the familiar confines of our comfort zones. It challenges our deeply held beliefs and values, forcing us to re-evaluate our worldview and our place in the world. This can be a daunting and uncomfortable process, triggering a range of emotions from anxiety and fear to excitement and anticipation.

Moreover, change often involves loss. It may mean letting go of old habits, relationships, or ways of life that have provided us with a sense of security and belonging. It may require us to acquire new skills or adapt to new technologies, which can be challenging and time-consuming. These losses, even if they pave the way for future gains,can be painful and difficult to accept, leading to resistance and a sense of nostalgia for the past.

However, it is precisely through these challenges and discomforts that we grow and evolve. Just as a muscle must be stretched and torn to grow stronger, so too must a society experience discomfort and disruption to evolve and progress.The growing pains we endure today are the harbingers of a brighter tomorrow. They are a sign that we are on the right path, that we are moving forward, that we are undergoing a profound transformation that will ultimately lead to a stronger, more resilient, and more prosperous nation.

Embracing the discomfort of growth requires a shift in mindset. It demands that we view challenges not as obstacles to be avoided, but as opportunities for learning and growth. It calls for us to cultivate resilience and adaptability, to develop the ability to navigate the inevitable ups and downs of the transformation journey with grace and determination. It requires us to embrace uncertainty, to be comfortable with not having all the answers, and to trust in our ability to adapt and overcome.

Furthermore, embracing the discomfort of growth requires strong leadership and effective communication. Leaders must be able to articulate a clear and compelling vision for the future, one that inspires hope and motivates people to embrace change. They must also be able to empathize with people's fears and concerns, to provide them with reassurance and support, and to demonstrate that the benefits of change outweigh the costs.

To achieve true metamorphosis, India must break free from the barriers that have long held it back, impeding its progress and limiting its potential. These barriers are both mental and structural, permeating all levels of society and hindering its ability to evolve and thrive in the 21st century.

Mental barriers encompass a wide range of outdated beliefs and attitudes that confine our potential and prevent us from embracing change. They include the fear of failure, which can paralyze us and prevent us from taking risks or pursuing our dreams. They include the resistance to change, which can blind us to new opportunities and possibilities. And they include the self-limiting belief that we are not capable of greatness, that we are somehow inferior or unworthy of success. These mental barriers, often deeply ingrained in our culture and psyche, can be just as confining as physical ones, and they must be dismantled if we are to realize our full potential as individuals and as a nation.

Structural barriers, on the other hand, are the tangible obstacles that impede progress and prevent us from achieving our goals. They include archaic laws and regulations that stifle innovation and entrepreneurship, entrenched power structures that perpetuate inequality and injustice, and systemic biases that discriminate against certain groups and individuals. These structural barriers create a playing field that is far from level, favoring the privileged few at the expense of the many. They create a system where opportunities are not equally distributed, where talent and merit are not always rewarded, and where the dreams of millions are crushed under the weight of systemic oppression.

Breaking these barriers, both mental and structural, is a monumental task, but it is one that India must undertake if it is to achieve true metamorphosis. It requires a concerted effort from all segments of society, from individuals to institutions, from the grassroots to the highest echelons of power.

At the individual level, breaking barriers begins with a change in mindset. It requires us to challenge our own limiting beliefs and assumptions, to embrace a growth mindset, and to cultivate a spirit of curiosity and experimentation. It means stepping outside our comfort zones, taking risks, and pursuing our dreams with passion and determination. It also involves supporting and empowering others to do the same, creating a culture of inclusivity and opportunity where everyone has the chance to succeed.

At the institutional level, breaking barriers requires a commitment to reform and innovation. It means updating outdated laws and regulations, dismantling entrenched power structures, and addressing systemic biases. It involves investing in education and training, promoting entrepreneurship and innovation, and creating a level playing field where everyone has a fair shot at success.

At the societal level, breaking barriers requires a collective effort to challenge the status quo and demand change. It means raising our voices against injustice and inequality, advocating for policies that promote inclusivity and opportunity, and holding our leaders accountable for their actions. It involves building bridges across communities, fostering dialogue and understanding, and working together to create a more just and equitable society for all.

The journey of breaking barriers will not be easy. It will require courage, resilience, and unwavering determination. It will involve confronting powerful forces that benefit from the status quo and resisting their attempts to maintain their grip on power. It will require us to overcome our own fears and insecurities, to challenge our own biases and prejudices, and to embrace the diversity and complexity of our society.

But the rewards of breaking barriers are immense. A society that is free from mental and structural barriers is a society that is truly liberated, a society where everyone has the opportunity to reach their full potential, regardless of their background or circumstances. It is a society that is dynamic, innovative, and prosperous, a society that is a beacon of hope and progress for the world.

India has a rich history of breaking barriers. From the struggle for independence to the fight for social justice, the Indian people have time and again demonstrated their courage and resilience in the face of adversity. They have shown that change is possible, even in the face of seemingly insurmountable challenges.

Today, India stands at another crossroads. The challenges we face are immense, but so too are the opportunities. By breaking free from the shackles of the past, by embracing change and innovation, and by working together to create a more just and equitable society, we can unleash India's full potential and usher in a new era of prosperity and progress.

The journey of transformation is not a smooth, linear path, but rather a dynamic and unpredictable voyage, filled with twists and turns, challenges and opportunities. To navigate this journey successfully, both individuals and society as a whole must cultivate adaptability and resilience - the twin pillars of navigating the winds of change.

Adaptability is the ability to adjust seamlessly to new situations and circumstances, to embrace change with open arms, and to thrive in an ever-evolving world. It is the willingness to acquire new skills, to embrace emerging technologies, and to evolve our ways of thinking and doing. In a world that is constantly changing at an unprecedented pace, driven by technological advancements, globalization, and shifting geopolitical realities, adaptability is not just desirable but essential for survival and success.

It requires us to be lifelong learners, constantly seeking out new knowledge and experiences, and to be open to new ideas and perspectives. It demands that we be flexible and agile, able to pivot and adapt our strategies as circumstances change. And it calls for us to be comfortable with ambiguity and uncertainty, to embrace the unknown and to see it not as a threat, but as a source of endless possibilities.

Resilience, on the other hand, is the ability to bounce back from adversity with renewed vigor, to weather the storms of change and emerge stronger and more determined. It is the inner strength to overcome challenges, to extract wisdom from our mistakes, and to keep moving forward, even when the going gets tough. In a world rife with uncertainty and change, resilience is the bedrock upon which we can build a strong and sustainable future.

It requires us to develop a growth mindset, to see setbacks not as failures but as opportunities for learning and growth. It calls for us to cultivate a sense of optimism and hope, to believe in our ability to overcome challenges and achieve our goals. And it demands that we build strong support networks, both within our families and communities, to provide us with the emotional and practical support we need to navigate the inevitable ups and downs of life.

Individuals can cultivate adaptability and resilience by adopting a growth mindset, embracing lifelong learning, and building strong support networks. They can also draw inspiration and learn from the experiences of others, both those who have achieved success and those who have faced setbacks. By studying the strategies and tactics that have enabled others to thrive in the face of change, individuals can gain valuable insights and develop their own toolkit for navigating the complexities of transformation.

Society as a whole can foster adaptability and resilience by investing in education, promoting innovation, and creating a safety net for those facing hardship. Education plays a critical role in equipping individuals with the knowledge and skills they need to adapt to a changing world. It fosters critical thinking, problem-solving, and creativity, enabling individuals to navigate complex challenges and seize new opportunities.

Promoting innovation is equally important, as it encourages individuals and organizations to experiment, take risks, and develop new solutions to emerging problems. It creates a culture of entrepreneurship and creativity, where new ideas are welcomed and nurtured, and where failure is seen not as a stigma but as a stepping stone to success.

Finally, creating a safety net for those facing hardship is essential for building a resilient society. It means providing support to those who are struggling, whether they are unemployed, sick, or facing other challenges. It involves creating a system where everyone has access to basic necessities such as food, shelter, and healthcare, and where everyone has the opportunity to rebuild their lives and contribute to society.

Change, though often accompanied by challenges and discomfort, is the lifeblood of survival and progress. It is the driving force behind evolution, the spark that ignites innovation, and the key to unlocking our boundless potential. It is the crucible in which societies are forged and reforged, where old paradigms give way to new possibilities, and where the seeds of a better future are sown.

India, poised like a butterfly on the brink of transformation, stands at the threshold of a remarkable metamorphosis. To realize its full potential and ascend to its rightful place among the world's leading nations, it must embrace change with open arms, shed its outdated paradigms, and emerge into a new era of possibilities. It must cast off the shackles of the past, break free from the limitations of its present, and soar towards a future that is brighter, bolder, and more inclusive.

This journey will not be without its trials. There will be obstacles and setbacks, moments of doubt and uncertainty, as the nation grapples with the complexities of change and navigates the uncharted waters of the future. There will be resistance from those who benefit from the status quo, who fear the loss of their power and privilege. There will be growing pains,as individuals and communities adjust to new realities and grapple with the inevitable disruptions that accompany transformation.

But if we can cultivate adaptability and resilience, if we can break free from the shackles of the past, and if we can unite in our pursuit of a more just and equitable society, then we can achieve a metamorphosis that will transform India into a beacon of hope and progress for the entire world. We can create a nation that is not only strong and prosperous but also compassionate and inclusive, a nation that embodies the values of democracy, diversity, and social justice.

The future is ours to shape. Let us embrace it with unwavering courage, unyielding determination, and an unshakeable belief in our own potential. Let us transform India into the nation it is destined to be - a nation that is not only a leader in the 21st century but also a model for the world, a nation that inspires others with its vision, its values, and its achievements.

Let us remember the butterfly, that humble creature that undergoes a remarkable transformation, emerging from its chrysalis with wings that carry it to new heights. Let us draw inspiration from its journey, its courage, and its resilience.And let us embark on our own metamorphosis, transforming India into a nation that soars, a nation that shines, a nation that fulfills its destiny and inspires the world.

This metamorphosis, this transformation of India, is not just a matter of policy changes or economic reforms, though these are undoubtedly important. It is also, and perhaps more fundamentally, a transformation of the human spirit. It is about unleashing the creativity, the passion, and the potential that lies within each and every one of us. It is about creating a society where every individual, regardless of their background or circumstances, has the opportunity to dream big, to pursue their passions, and to contribute to the collective good.

It is about fostering a culture of innovation and entrepreneurship, where new ideas are welcomed and nurtured, and where failure is seen not as a stigma but as a stepping stone to success. It is about investing in education and research,empowering our young people with the knowledge and skills they need to thrive in the 21st century. And it is about creating a society that values compassion and empathy, where we care for the most vulnerable among us and work together to build a more just and equitable world.

This transformation will not happen overnight. It will require sustained effort and commitment from all of us, from the highest levels of government to the grassroots of our society. It will require us to challenge outdated beliefs and practices,to embrace new technologies and ideas, and to work together to build a better future for ourselves and for generations to come.

But the journey, though challenging, is also filled with immense possibilities. It is a journey that can lead us to a future where India is not just a rising power, but a shining example of what a nation can achieve when it embraces change,unleashes its potential, and works together to create a better world for all. It is a journey that can lead us to a future where India is not just a land of ancient wisdom and rich traditions, but also a land of innovation, creativity, and progress.

Let us embark on this journey with hope and determination. Let us embrace the challenges and opportunities that lie ahead. And let us work together to transform India into a nation that not only fulfills its own destiny but also inspires the world.

This metamorphosis, this transformation of India, is not merely a theoretical concept or a distant dream. It is a living,breathing reality that is unfolding before our very eyes. Across the length and breadth of our nation, we see signs of change, glimmers of hope, and a growing sense of possibility.

We see it in the young entrepreneurs who are harnessing the power of technology to create innovative solutions to pressing problems. We see it in the scientists and researchers who are pushing the boundaries of knowledge and discovery. We see it in the artists and writers who are challenging conventional norms and expressing new perspectives.And we see it in the countless ordinary citizens who are working tirelessly to make a difference in their communities, to build a better future for themselves and their families.

These individuals, these change-makers, are the true heroes of India's transformation. They are the ones who are leading the charge, who are inspiring others with their vision, their passion, and their unwavering commitment to progress. They are the ones who are proving that change is possible, that India can indeed achieve greatness.

But their efforts alone are not enough. To truly transform India, we need a collective effort, a movement that encompasses all segments of society. We need the government to create an enabling environment, to invest in education and infrastructure, and to remove the barriers that impede progress. We need the private sector to innovate and create jobs, to invest in research and development, and to contribute to the social good. And we need civil society to hold both the government and the private sector accountable, to advocate for the rights of the marginalized, and to ensure that the benefits of development are shared by all.

This is a call to action, a call to all Indians to join hands and work together to transform our nation. It is a call to embrace change, to unleash our potential, and to build a future that is worthy of our dreams and aspirations. It is a call to rise above the challenges and obstacles that we face, to overcome the divisions that have long plagued our society,and to create a nation that is united in its pursuit of progress and prosperity.

The journey ahead will not be easy, but it is a journey that we must undertake. It is a journey that will test our resolve,challenge our assumptions, and push us to the limits of our capabilities. But it is also a journey that is filled with hope and promise, a journey that can lead us to a future where India is not just a rising power, but a shining beacon of hope and progress for the world.

Let us embark on this journey with courage, determination, and an unwavering belief in our ability to achieve greatness. Let us transform India into a nation that not only fulfills its own destiny but also inspires the world. Let us create a future that is worthy of our children and grandchildren, a future that is filled with hope, opportunity, and endless possibilities.

The time for change is now. The future of India is in our hands. Let us seize this moment and create a metamorphosis that will transform our nation and shape the world.

The Odyssey

The familiar hum of the engine, the rhythmic swish of the windshield wipers against the light drizzle, the muted glow of the dashboard – it all blended into a comforting symphony as Parth navigated the winding roads of Patiala. His hands, once scarred and bandaged, now confidently gripped the steering wheel, a testament to his resilience and the remarkable journey he had undertaken.

As he drove, his thoughts drifted, carried by the wind and the melancholic rhythm of the rain. He thought of his parents,their unwavering love and support as a constant beacon in his life. He thought of Mohini, her fierce spirit and unwavering belief in him a source of endless inspiration. He thought of Dr. Madhav, his wisdom and compassion a guiding light on his path to self-discovery.

The landscape blurred past his window, a tapestry of green fields, bustling villages, and ancient temples. Each sight evoked a memory, a fragment of his past woven into the fabric of his present. He saw himself as a child, running barefoot through the fields, his laughter echoing through the air. He saw himself as a teenager, grappling with the pressures of exams and societal expectations, his dreams seemingly slipping through his fingers. He saw himself on that fateful night, his life hanging in the balance, his future shrouded in darkness.

But amidst the shadows, he also saw glimmers of light. He saw the unwavering support of his family, the kindness of strangers, the resilience of the human spirit. He saw the opportunities that lay before him, the endless possibilities that awaited his embrace.

The road ahead stretched before him, a metaphor for the journey he had yet to travel. It was a journey filled with both challenges and triumphs, setbacks and breakthroughs. But Parth was no longer afraid. He had faced his demons,embraced his vulnerabilities, and emerged stronger, wiser, and more determined than ever before.

He thought of his company, a testament to his passion for sustainability and his commitment to making a positive impact on the world. He thought of the countless lives he had touched, the communities he had empowered, the environment he had helped protect.

As the rain intensified, Parth slowed down, his gaze fixed on the road ahead. He knew that the journey was far from over. There would be more obstacles to overcome, more battles to fight. But he was ready. He had found his purpose, and he would pursue it with unwavering dedication.

The windshield wipers continued their rhythmic dance, clearing the path ahead. And as Parth drove on, a sense of peace settled over him. He was no longer a victim of circumstance, but a master of his own destiny. He was Parth, the survivor, the entrepreneur, the dreamer. And his odyssey had just begun.

Just as the legendary hero Odysseus embarked on a perilous journey filled with trials and tribulations, so too do we all embark on our own personal odysseys through life. Our paths may not be filled with mythical creatures and vengeful gods, but they are nonetheless fraught with challenges, uncertainties, and the constant pursuit of happiness and fulfillment. Like Odysseus, we navigate through uncharted waters, encounter unexpected obstacles, and strive to reach our Ithaca, that elusive destination that represents our ultimate goals and aspirations.

This chapter invites us to reflect on the nature of this journey, to explore the complexities of happiness and fulfillment,and to understand the challenges that come with their pursuit. It draws inspiration from the timeless themes of "The Odyssey," using the metaphor of a long and winding journey to illuminate the path towards a life well-lived. It encourages us to embrace the journey itself, to appreciate the lessons learned along the way, and to find meaning and purpose in the pursuit of our dreams.

Happiness, that elusive and often fleeting state of being, has been the subject of philosophical inquiry, psychological research, and cultural exploration for centuries. It is a concept that is both universal and deeply personal, with different individuals and societies defining it in diverse and sometimes contradictory ways.

From a philosophical perspective, happiness has been interpreted as the pursuit of virtue and the attainment of a harmonious balance between reason and emotion. It has been seen as the ultimate goal of human existence, the culmination of a life well-lived.

Psychological perspectives, on the other hand, often focus on the subjective experience of happiness, exploring the factors that contribute to positive emotions, well-being, and life satisfaction. They emphasize the importance of individual differences in temperament, personality, and coping mechanisms in shaping our experience of happiness.

Cultural perspectives add another layer of complexity to the understanding of happiness. Different cultures have their own unique conceptions of what constitutes a good life and what brings happiness and fulfillment. In the Indian context, happiness is often intertwined with spiritual concepts such as dharma, karma, and moksha. It is seen as a state of inner peace and contentment that arises from living in accordance with one's purpose and contributing to the well-being of others.

While there is no single, universally accepted definition of happiness, there are certain common threads that run through these diverse perspectives. Happiness is often associated with a sense of purpose and meaning in life, with positive relationships and social connections, with the pursuit of personal growth and development, and with the ability to cope with challenges and adversity.

Living a healthy, fulfilled life involves cultivating these elements of happiness, both individually and collectively. It requires us to be mindful of our thoughts and emotions, to nurture our relationships, to pursue our passions, and to contribute to the well-being of our communities. It also involves recognizing that happiness is not a static state, but a dynamic and evolving process that requires constant effort and adaptation.

The pursuit of happiness and success is rarely a smooth and effortless path. It is often fraught with challenges, setbacks,and moments of doubt and despair. History, literature, and contemporary life are replete with examples of individuals who have overcome immense obstacles and adversity to achieve their goals and find fulfillment. These stories remind us that struggle is not an impediment to happiness and success, but rather an integral part of the journey.

Literature, too, offers countless examples of the role of struggle in the pursuit of happiness and success. From the epic journeys of Odysseus and Aeneas to the coming-of-age stories of Jane Eyre and Holden Caulfield, literature is filled with characters who navigate through challenges, overcome obstacles, and emerge transformed by their experiences.These stories remind us that the journey itself, with all its twists and turns, is as important as the destination.

In contemporary life, we see examples of struggle all around us. From the entrepreneur who faces countless rejections before finally securing funding for their startup, to the athlete who overcomes injuries and setbacks to achieve their Olympic dreams, to the single parent who juggles multiple jobs and responsibilities to provide for their family, struggle is a universal human experience.

Embracing the journey, rather than just focusing on the destination, is key to finding a deeper sense of satisfaction and accomplishment. It is in the midst of struggle that we discover our true potential, that we develop the skills and resilience needed to overcome challenges, and that we forge a deeper connection with our purpose and values.

Moreover, struggle can also lead to a greater appreciation of the joys and successes that we experience along the way. It is often through overcoming adversity that we learn to savor the moments of triumph, to cherish the relationships that sustain us, and to find gratitude for the opportunities that life presents us.

Of course, embracing struggle does not mean seeking out hardship or pain. It means recognizing that challenges are an inevitable part of life and that they can be opportunities for growth and transformation. It means cultivating a mindset of resilience and perseverance, of learning from our mistakes and setbacks, and of never giving up on our dreams.

That being said though, it's important to remember that struggles doesn't sell well. Society does not acknowledge, let alone appreciate struggle, until you're successful. On the bright side though, what exactly is success is something you have all permission to decide.

Furthermore, it means finding meaning and purpose in the journey itself, in the lessons learned, the relationships forged, and the impact we have on others. It means recognizing that happiness and success are not just about reaching the destination, but also about the journey we take to get there.

By embracing the journey, with all its challenges and uncertainties, we can create a life that is not only fulfilling but also rich in meaning and purpose. We can discover our true potential, forge deeper connections with others, and make a lasting impact on the world. We can transform our struggles into stepping stones towards a brighter future, and in doing so, we can truly live a life well-lived.

In the relentless pursuit of happiness and success, it is easy to lose sight of the importance of balance. Modern society,with its emphasis on achievement and material wealth, often encourages us to push ourselves to the limit, to strive for ever-higher goals, and to never settle for anything less than the best. This relentless pursuit, while admirable in its drive and ambition, can often lead to an imbalance, a tilting of the scales that leaves us feeling stressed, anxious, and unfulfilled.

While ambition and drive are undoubtedly important qualities, they must be tempered with contentment and a sense of inner peace. The constant striving for more, the relentless pursuit of external validation, can leave us feeling empty and disconnected from our true selves. It can lead to a sense of perpetual dissatisfaction, where no achievement is ever enough, and where happiness always seems to be just out of reach.

The tension between personal goals and societal expectations can further exacerbate this imbalance. On the one hand,we are driven by our own dreams and aspirations, our desire to achieve something meaningful and leave our mark on the world. On the other hand, we are constantly bombarded with messages about what we should be doing, what we should be achieving, and how we should be living our lives. These external pressures can create a sense of inadequacy and dissatisfaction, even when we are making progress towards our own goals. We may find ourselves comparing our achievements to those of others, feeling pressured to conform to societal norms, and sacrificing our own happiness in the pursuit of external validation.

Finding balance in life requires us to navigate this tension with wisdom and discernment. It means recognizing that happiness and fulfillment are not solely dependent on external achievements, but also on our internal state of being. It involves cultivating a sense of contentment with what we have, while also striving to reach our full potential. It is about finding the sweet spot between ambition and contentment, between pushing ourselves to grow and evolve, and accepting ourselves for who we are in the present moment.

One way to achieve this balance is through mindfulness and self-reflection. By taking the time to pause, to observe our thoughts and emotions without judgment, and to connect with our inner selves, we can gain a deeper understanding of our true needs and desires. This self-awareness can help us to make choices that are aligned with our values and priorities, rather than being driven by external pressures or expectations. It can also help us to cultivate a sense of gratitude and appreciation for the good things in our lives, which can be a powerful antidote to the constant striving for more.

Another important aspect of finding balance is setting meaningful priorities. It is essential to identify what truly matters to us, what brings us joy and fulfillment, and what contributes to our overall well-being. This may involve re-evaluating our goals and aspirations, letting go of those that no longer serve us, and focusing our time and energy on those that truly resonate with our hearts and souls. By setting meaningful priorities, we can create a life that is both successful and satisfying, a life that is in harmony with our values and aspirations.

Moreover, finding balance requires us to be mindful of our physical and mental health. Our bodies and minds are interconnected, and neglecting one can have a detrimental impact on the other. It is important to take care of our bodies through exercise, healthy eating, and adequate rest. It is equally important to nurture our minds through mindfulness practices, stress management techniques, and seeking support when needed. By prioritizing our physical and mental health, we can create a strong foundation for a balanced and fulfilling life.

Finally, finding balance involves cultivating a sense of connection and belonging. We are social beings, and our relationships with others play a crucial role in our happiness and well-being. It is important to nurture our relationships with family and friends, to build strong communities, and to contribute to the greater good. By fostering a sense of connection and belonging, we can create a sense of purpose and meaning in our lives that transcends individual achievements and material possessions.

The art of balance is a lifelong practice, one that requires constant effort and adjustment. It is about finding the sweet spot between ambition and contentment, between striving for our goals and appreciating the journey. It is about creating a life that is both meaningful and fulfilling, a life that is in harmony with our values and priorities. It is about embracing the complexities and contradictions of the human experience, and finding a way to navigate them with grace, wisdom, and compassion.

Life is a journey, an odyssey filled with challenges, opportunities, and endless possibilities. It is a journey that takes us through uncharted waters, tests our resilience, and pushes us to the limits of our capabilities. But it is also a journey that is filled with beauty, wonder, and the potential for profound growth and fulfillment. It is a journey that is uniquely ours,shaped by our choices, our experiences, and our interactions with the world around us.

Happiness and success are not endpoints, but evolving states of being. They are not destinations that we reach once and for all, but rather companions that we cultivate and nurture along the way. They are the fruits of a life well-lived, a life that is marked by purpose, meaning, and a deep connection to our true selves. They are not about achieving some external standard of perfection, but about living in alignment with our values, pursuing our passions, and contributing to the world in a way that is meaningful to us.

As we navigate our personal odysseys, let us embrace the journey with courage and wisdom. Let us recognize that the path itself is as important as the goals we strive to achieve. Let us find joy in the challenges, learn from our setbacks,and celebrate our victories, big and small. Let us cultivate a sense of curiosity and wonder, always open to new experiences and perspectives. And let us remember that the journey is not a solitary one, but a shared experience that connects us to others and to the world around us.

The road ahead may be long and winding, but it holds the potential for profound growth and fulfillment. It is a path that can lead us to a deeper understanding of ourselves, our relationships, and our place in the world. It is a path that can lead us to a life of purpose, meaning, and lasting happiness.

Let us embark on this journey with open hearts and open minds, ready to embrace the unknown and to discover the treasures that lie within. Let us navigate the challenges with courage and resilience, and let us celebrate the joys and successes with gratitude and humility.

For in the end, it is not the destination that matters most, but the journey itself, the odyssey that shapes us, transforms us, and ultimately leads us to a life of happiness and fulfillment. It is a journey that is worth taking, a journey that is uniquely ours, and a journey that has the power to transform not only ourselves but also the world around us.

This journey, this odyssey of India's transformation, is not a solitary one. It is a shared endeavor, a collective voyage that involves every citizen, every community, and every institution. It is a journey that calls for collaboration,cooperation, and a shared commitment to building a better future for all.

Just as Odysseus relied on the support of his loyal crew and the guidance of the gods, so too must India rely on the collective wisdom and strength of its people to navigate the challenges and opportunities that lie ahead. It is a journey that requires us to transcend our differences, to bridge the divides that have long plagued our society, and to work together towards a common goal.

This collective effort begins with recognizing the interconnectedness of our destinies. We are all part of a larger whole,and our individual actions and choices have a ripple effect that extends far beyond ourselves. Whether we are a farmer in a remote village, a teacher in a bustling city, or a policymaker in the halls of power, we all have a role to play in shaping the future of our nation.

It is a journey that calls for us to embrace diversity, to celebrate the richness and plurality of our culture, and to recognize that our strength lies in our differences. It is a journey that demands that we uphold the values of democracy,justice, and equality, and that we strive to create a society where everyone has the opportunity to reach their full potential, regardless of their caste, creed, gender, or socioeconomic background.

This journey also requires us to be mindful of our impact on the planet and to embrace sustainable practices that ensure the well-being of future generations. It is a journey that calls for us to be responsible stewards of our natural resources,to protect our environment, and to promote a harmonious coexistence between humans and nature.

As we embark on this journey, let us remember the words of the ancient Indian poet, Rabindranath Tagore, who wrote,"Let my thoughts come to you, when I am gone, like the afterglow of sunset at the margin of starry silence." Let us strive to create a future that is worthy of his words, a future that is filled with hope, beauty, and the promise of a better tomorrow.

Let us embrace the odyssey, with all its challenges and opportunities, and let us work together to build a nation that is not only prosperous and powerful but also compassionate and just. Let us create a future where every Indian can live a life of dignity, purpose, and fulfillment. Let us transform India into a nation that not only fulfills its own destiny but also inspires the world.

The time for change is now. The future of India is in our hands. Let us seize this moment and create a metamorphosis that will transform our nation and shape the world.

Afterword

Writing this book has been an odyssey of its own, a journey that has taken me deep into the heart of India's healthcare and education systems, and, by extension, into the very soul of our nation. What began as a mere curiosity, a desire to understand the persistent challenges in these sectors, soon grew into a profound commitment to unravel the complexities and propose pathways to a brighter future. This book is the culmination of that journey, and it represents not just an intellectual exercise but an emotional and personal quest for solutions.

From the outset, I knew that the issues I would confront were neither new nor simple. The challenges that beset India's healthcare and education systems are as old as the nation itself, entrenched in a history of colonialism, economic disparity, and political inertia. Yet, as I delved deeper into my research, I found that beneath the surface of despair, there existed a remarkable resilience – a resilience born from the efforts of countless individuals who, despite the odds, have dedicated their lives to making a difference. This book is as much about them as it is about the problems they face.

One of the most daunting aspects of writing this book was the sheer scale of the issues at hand. Healthcare and education are vast, multifaceted systems, each with its own set of challenges and opportunities. At times, the enormity of the task felt overwhelming. How does one do justice to the stories of millions of people who struggle daily within these systems? How can the narrative capture the complexity of the issues without losing the reader in a sea of statistics and jargon? These were questions that haunted me throughout the writing process.

Another challenge was the emotional toll of confronting the harsh realities of our systems. Writing about the healthcare crisis in rural India, for instance, was not just a matter of gathering data; it was about listening to the stories of those who have lost loved ones to preventable diseases, of doctors who work tirelessly in understaffed clinics, and of communities that have been left behind by the march of progress. Similarly, the chapters on education forced me to grapple with the pressures faced by students, the mental health crisis among our youth, and the systemic flaws that stifle creativity and innovation.

Yet, despite these challenges, this journey has also been one of hope. For every story of despair, there is a story of resilience; for every challenge, there is a potential solution waiting to be realized. This book is my attempt to shine a light on both the darkness and the light, to offer not just a critique of our systems, but a roadmap for change.

Throughout this book, I have tried to explore the two pillars upon which any nation stands: healthcare and education. These are not just sectors; they are the very foundations of a society's well-being and progress. If these pillars are weak, the entire structure is at risk of collapse.

In the chapters on healthcare, we journeyed through the labyrinth of India's medical system, confronting the stark reality of a nation where access to quality healthcare is still a privilege rather than a right. We explored the urban-rural divide, the challenges faced by healthcare professionals, and the systemic inefficiencies that plague the system. Yet, we also looked at the potential for transformation – the promise of technology, the impact of successful public health campaigns, and the dedication of those who work tirelessly to heal the nation. The message is clear: while the challenges are immense, they are not insurmountable. With the right policies, investments, and political will, India can build a healthcare system that serves all its citizens, regardless of their socio-economic status or geographic location.

Education, the second pillar, is equally critical. In the chapters dedicated to this theme, we examined the pressures faced by students, the flaws in our curriculum, and the societal expectations that often crush the spirit of our youth. We discussed the need for systemic reform, the potential of new educational models, and the importance of mental health and well-being in the academic environment. Education is not just about imparting knowledge; it is about nurturing the minds and souls of the next generation. If we are to unlock India's potential, we must first unlock the potential of its students. This requires a shift in how we view education – from a rigid, exam-oriented system to one that fosters creativity, critical thinking, and emotional intelligence.

Throughout both themes, a common thread emerges: the need for systemic change. Whether it is healthcare or education, the problems we face are deeply rooted in the structures that govern these systems. To effect meaningful change, we must be willing to confront these structures, to question the status quo, and to advocate for bold, transformative reforms.

The title of this book, "Chakr," is not just a metaphor; it is a symbol of the cyclical nature of time and change, a reminder that history is not linear but circular. In choosing this title, I was inspired by the Sudarshan Chakra, a powerful symbol in Indian mythology. The Sudarshan Chakra is not just a weapon; it is a symbol of righteousness, protection, and the eternal cycle of creation and destruction. In the context of this book, it represents the idea that change is both inevitable and necessary – that in order to build a better future, we must be willing to confront and dismantle the systems that no longer serve us.

The cycle of change, like the spinning of a chakra, is continuous and dynamic. It is not enough to simply identify the problems; we must also be willing to take action, to initiate the cycle of transformation that will lead to a more just and equitable society. This book is my contribution to that cycle – a call to action for all who read it to become agents of change in their own lives and communities.

The Sudarshan Chakra also serves as a reminder of the power of righteousness. In our pursuit of progress, we must never lose sight of the principles that guide us – justice, equity, and compassion. These are the values that should underpin our healthcare and education systems, and they are the values that will guide us as we work to build a better future.

As we conclude this journey together, I want to leave you with a vision for the future – a vision of an India that has embraced the changes proposed in this book, an India where healthcare is accessible, education is empowering, and societal structures are just and equitable.

This vision is not a utopia; it is a possibility. But it is a possibility that requires collective effort and political will. It requires us to move beyond the rhetoric of reform and to take concrete actions that will make a difference in the lives of ordinary people. This is not just the responsibility of the government; it is the responsibility of every citizen, every institution, and every community.

The path forward is not easy. It will require difficult choices, bold decisions, and the willingness to challenge entrenched interests. But it is a path worth taking, because the rewards are immense. A healthier, better-educated population is not just an end in itself; it is the foundation of a prosperous, innovative, and resilient nation.

Collaboration is key to this transformation. The government, the private sector, civil society, and individuals must all work together to create the conditions for change. This means investing in healthcare and education, prioritizing the needs of the most vulnerable, and ensuring that everyone has access to the opportunities they need to succeed. It also means fostering a culture of accountability and transparency, where decisions are made based on evidence and the best interests of the people.

In envisioning the future, I am reminded of the words of Mahatma Gandhi: "The best way to find yourself is to lose yourself in the service of others." This book is an invitation to lose ourselves in the service of a greater cause – the cause of creating a better India. It is a call to action for all who read it to take up the mantle of change, to become champions of reform, and to work tirelessly to build a future that is just, equitable, and full of promise.

As I close this book, I want to express my heartfelt gratitude to all those who have supported me throughout this journey. To my mentors, whose guidance and encouragement have been invaluable; to my family, whose patience and understanding have been a constant source of strength; and to my readers, whose interest in these critical issues has been a driving force behind this work.

I also want to extend my gratitude to the countless individuals who have shared their stories, their insights, and their experiences with me. Your voices have been the heart of this book, and it is my hope that your stories will inspire others to join in the effort to create positive change.

To you, the reader, I offer my deepest thanks for embarking on this journey with me. I hope that this book has provided you with valuable insights, inspired you to think critically about the issues facing our nation, and motivated you to take action. The future of India is in our hands, and together, we can build a brighter, more equitable future for all.

Thank you for your time, your passion, and your commitment to a better India. May the lessons of this book inspire you to become a beacon of change in your own sphere of influence.

With deepest gratitude and hope,

Jai Hind

About the Author

Utkarsh Luthra is the founder and CEO of Medoc Health. He handles the overall operations and execution of the company along with all internal and external stakeholders affairs. He is an expert in System Design and Execution along with Project Management.

Medoc Health offers affordable, comprehensive AI-powered tools for doctors and integrated management solutions for hospitals and clinics, emphasizing user-friendliness and customization. Medoc's objective is to ease the access to medicine and medical finances while also being transparent and connected to their end users and patient families. They focus on inclusivity of all and convenience with AI Systems in place to help doctors move from traditional methods to methods which are better than paper.

Utkarsh is a patron of entrepreneurship and youth development and understands that it is important to take action instead of just stating issues. He has mentored over 50 ideation startups and 700+ students in Software Development.

In his free time, Utkarsh loves to read, play his guitar and engage in conversations with people to learn more about them.